why you must start your own business now

EMPTY NEST EGG

Second Edition

Terry Noel

EMPTY NEST EGG © 2009, 2011 by Terry Noel.

Graphic design and illustration by Dena McDonald

Printed in the United States.

Dedication

To my father, Paul A. Noel, who taught me that the mirror is the most honest friend I will ever have.

Disclaimer

Table of Contents

1

Foreword

In the first edition of this book, I told you that we were in for a rough ride. I was wrong. We are in for an economic disaster. In late 2008 and early 2009, we came within hours (literally) of having the global financial system shut down completely. Through a set of maneuvers that boggle the mind, the United States government bailed out some of our largest financial institutions and insurance companies. Oh, and they made all of us proud owners of a large chunk of the auto-manufacturing industry as well.

Some say that without the bailout we would now be in the middle of a catastrophe worse than the Great Depression. Even if that were true, which I doubt, the bailouts only postponed our day of reckoning. Are we really better off skirting one disaster for a worse one later?

It is now the fall of 2010. We were recently informed that the Great Recession officially ended in 2009, but no one is celebrating. The unemployment rate is still high, and there is little prospect of business expansion—people are nervous and unsure. The Federal Reserve is pumping even more money into the system, raising fears of inflation. Where is the good news?

I still believe that within all this apparent chaos, there is hope. A powerful engine has been building steam for the last thirty years— entrepreneurship. Long before the big banks, automakers, and insurance companies started going bankrupt, our economy was transforming itself into a small business economy.

This is good news for people who are willing to learn how to start a new business. If your only answer to the question, "How do I make a living?" is "Get a job," you may be in for a rude shock. Hopefully, you still have your job if you have been working. You may even get to keep it. But can you really convince yourself that your job is the answer to your financial future? To your retirement? To your children's future?

Are you retired already? Do you believe your savings will keep you going even if you live longer than expected? During the writing of this second edition, my grandmother turned 100. What if you beat Grandma in longevity? Starting a business may have been the last thing on your mind when you retired. What about now?

This book was inspired by an ongoing passion of mine—how to teach entrepreneurship in a way that makes a real difference in the lives of real people. I earned my Ph.D. in 1997, and it remains one of my proudest accomplishments. But it was not my doctoral education that gave me the tools to educate and inspire people to build businesses. It was the real experiences I had in my private life.

When I was twenty-four years old, I was still a farmer. I had grown up on the family farm and had a sound work ethic. Although farming had its appeal, it had become apparent that it was not going to be my life's calling. While pondering what to do with the rest of my life, I had the opportunity to open my own martial arts school. The chance to go out on my own was thrilling, and I gave it everything I had. I also lost everything I had. Everything.

Later on, I did figure out a way to earn good money teaching martial arts, but my initial failure haunted me for years. How could that happen? I was bright, energetic and sincere. I worked hard, was honest, and did all the "right" things (at least as I understood those things then), yet I still got clobbered. That was not supposed to happen to me. It was supposed to happen to lazy and stupid people. I felt, well, lazy and stupid.

It took me many years to realize that while I had a good education, there was one important element missing. I was woefully ignorant of how entrepreneurship actually works. My "illumination" came not in a flash, but over a period of years. During my stay at one university, I had the chance to put together half of a dozen or so investment deals for a one million dollar student venture fund. Prepping and advising entrepreneurs, getting sets of investors to agree among themselves and with the entrepreneurs on terms, and actually launching the business were invaluable experiences.

At another institution, I had the chance to serve as a coach for entrepreneurs preparing to make presentations at a twice-yearly venture capital conference. Listening to bright investors and entrepreneurs regularly gave me powerful insights into what makes a successful entrepreneurial business tick.

I came to two conclusions. First, many entrepreneurs, even those who have gained some traction in the marketplace and are ready to grow, do not know much about business, especially finance. I have seen accomplished entrepreneurs stammer and stutter when asked to provide even the simplest accounting of how an investor's money would be used to create more money (that is, provide a return of and a return on investment). Most could go on and on (and on) about their product or service. Most could tell heroic tales of how they scraped together enough money to get as far as they had gotten. But when it came down to the nuts and bolts of designing and implementing a viable business model, they were lost.

Second, I discovered that successful entrepreneurs sure know how to screw up. Most of the people I have met who have achieved great success have experienced at least one, and usually several, unmitigated disasters. Yet they kept coming back for more. How do you teach that kind of thing?

Through years of experimentation in my classes, absorbing lessons from real people doing real business, and starting my own businesses, I have come up with a method for teaching entrepreneurship basics. The book is designed to take you up to the point of business launch: how to get an idea, evaluate it, and put it into action. Alone, it will give you indispensable entrepreneurial skills.

Some of you will want to dig deeper. For you, I provide online courses on my web site, **entrescape.com**. Each module takes you through a series of lessons and exercises that expand on what you will learn in this book.

Enjoy, and welcome to your future.

1 Well, How Did We Get Here?

"You may ask yourself,
'Well, how did I get here?'"
—*Talking Heads*

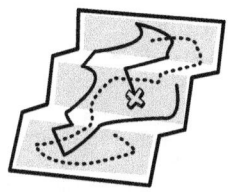 I have always been an optimist, and I keep a couple of pessimistic friends just to remind me why I am an optimist. They delight in ribbing me about generally expecting the best. I just laugh along with them, knowing that ninety-nine percent of the terrible things they fear never come to pass. Conspiracy theories, tainted food, secret government plots—all the usual list of doom-sayers' dire predictions serve to amuse more than frighten me.

Something has changed in the last three years. For the first time in my life, I am genuinely worried about the United States as a nation and about the world in general. Recent events have challenged my optimism more than ever before. As I wrote the first edition of this book, the housing market had started its meltdown. The stock market had just had its worst week in over one hundred years. Financial institutions were failing in droves. The auto industry had just received a bailout. Nest eggs that people had worked years to build were crumbling into dust.

Since then, what has happened? Is there any reason to believe we learned anything? Is there any reason to shed my pessimism for a rosier view of the future?

The truth is, we are in deeper trouble now than we were three years ago. The worst threats are being masked by government and the media and largely ignored by the public. The story of what actually happened during the Big Crisis has now emerged, and it has become clear how close we were to a complete global meltdown. Every attempt to put lipstick on this pig has resulted in a more confident but considerably uglier pig.

I had known that economic problems were headed our way for several years. This is not because I am any better than anyone else at predicting the future. I just know how to add and subtract. Projections for Social Security and Medicare show clearly that politicians have promised things to future generations that they cannot possibly deliver. Being an optimist, I hoped beyond hope that as the time of reckoning grew near, our leaders would stop to reconsider the insanity of continuing to spend, spend, spend while simultaneously killing the engine of prosperity—free markets. I figured somehow, some way, Congress would realize that the bizarre set of regulations they generate daily were killing America's businesses and enriching those who seek government favors over genuine competition. I just knew we would wake up.

I was wrong.

Our government is addicted to deficit spending. Spending increases year to year *no matter what.* This is not news, really. Both Republicans and Democrats have been overspending in government for years. What astonishes me is that President Barack Obama's administration felt obliged to pass a health care bill about which we know only one thing for sure—that it will break the bank.

And before you get to feeling too smug, remember that we the people have allowed them to get away with this. Why? Simple. It is because as more and more groups stand to benefit from government largess or from decreased competition through tariffs, skewed regulations, and government-sponsored monopolies, the more likely it is that voters will put people in office who promise the sun, moon and stars. Neat racket, huh?

The making of a disaster

This is not a book on politics. It is a book about taking action to secure your future. Nonetheless, it is important to understand *why* our economy has become so unstable. Building wealth from the rubble that will be left after the current debacle will require an unswerving dedication to reality and to the true principles of capitalism, which have long been forgotten by most of the general public.

I believe that three major factors have set us up for a disaster. And I don't mean the bailout. That one is a mere tremor compared to the earthquake that will shake all our teeth out if we do not make major changes in our economic system. The first occurred seventy years ago during the 1930s. President Franklin Roosevelt, seeing a nation in shambles after the great stock market crash of 1929, established a series of government programs designed to bolster the economy and help Joe and Jane Citizen to get out of the soup line and back to work.

The problem was, Roosevelt was basing his remedies on an economic theory that appeared to work in the short run but had disastrous long-term consequences. Keynesian economics advocated deficit spending to boost the economy. Keynes's reasoning was that when economies lagged, people needed to be given more money to spend. That does indeed work, but only in an illusionary fashion. In the end, all the newly printed dollars that are injected into the economy by government devalue those already in circulation. Decades later, we are reaping what we sowed. Inflation, even at the low rates we are experiencing now, eats away the value of every dollar we earn.

In addition to deficit spending, the Roosevelt era saw the creation of government programs designed to help people survive economically into old age. Thus, Social Security. Even those people who think that government *should* be in the business of providing retirement benefits—I am not one of them—have to admit that something has gone terribly wrong. In 1940, there were 160 workers for every retiree. Today there are 3.3 (Social Security Administration). In a few years, government will no longer be able to honor its promises without large tax increases and/or reduced benefits. And even if they do continue to issue the checks, it is likely that rampant inflation will eat away the purchasing power of seniors (from an interview with Congressman Ron Paul, goldsilver.com).

The second major event in our economic demise occurred in 1971. President Richard Nixon took the U.S. off the gold standard, effectively removing any pretense that the dollar was backed by any tangible asset. The crux of the issue is this—money "works" only as long as people believe in it. The paper that you and I carry around has no intrinsic value. It has value only if all of us who use it believe that it can be traded in the future for things we can use, like food, shelter, and clothing.

Gold is different. Even though it has little intrinsic value (for example as an efficient conductor of electricity) it has historically been thought of as "real" money. One reason is that the total supply of gold in the world grows very slowly. For all practical purposes, it is constant.

For that reason—and because its purity is easily determined—gold naturally evolved as a standard of exchange. It became a standard not because any government *decreed* it to be money, but because people in general *recognized* it as money. Big difference.

The problem with gold is that it is heavy and hard to carry around. Paper money evolved as a way to represent gold. As long as people using paper money knew that it could be exchanged for actual gold, that system worked fine. The United States government at one time issued its currency on that basis. A paper dollar could be exchanged for its gold equivalent.

Alas, though, politicians lie awake at night thinking up ways to get something for nothing. In a series of steps that began with the establishment of the Federal Reserve System in 1913, the United States went off the gold standard. Money gradually came to be thought of as the paper itself rather than gold. Nixon's unilateral move in 1971 was just the last nail in the coffin. Over that period of time, the government developed a habit of creating paper money to buy all the things politicians like to buy, like votes. As more paper money circulates, its value drops.

Eventually, such a system cannot hold up. The whole economy becomes based upon a fiction—the fiction of fiat (government-decreed) money. When certain sets of events occur together, like housing market declines and bankruptcies in large companies, there is a general panic. The instability of the system hurts you and me because we plan on retiring and living on money we thought would have value. If the system crashes, we suffer.

The third trend has been an addiction to jobs. Over the past several decades, there has been a strong trend away from self-employment (Bureau of Labor Statistics). As business organizations grew in size during the first part of the twentieth century, more jobs became available, and there occurred a drift toward the nine-to-five routine, trading time on the job for money.

None of this was bad *per se*. The rise of the large organization was beneficial in countless ways. Jobs were created, consumer goods became more widely available and wealth increased dramatically. People live better now than at any point in human history. The problem is not the fact that more people have jobs as opposed to being self-employed—it is that we have forgotten how to run businesses on our own. We have learned to rely exclusively upon others for our livelihoods.

The tendency to show up at work, collect a paycheck and hope for promotions worked, for a while. As long as large businesses were relatively stable and technology did not change too rapidly, the world chugged along just fine. We are learning now that this is not a permanent condition. Large businesses are failing or downsizing, leaving employees stranded. Old skills are no longer needed, forcing people to learn fast or die poor. The world has changed, leaving us no choice but to change in response.

Retirement

Along with the job instability we see in today's economy comes another issue—retirement. One part of this problem stems from the simple fact that we live longer than we used to. Many of us want to live out our last years enjoying the fruits of our labor. Longer periods of retirement mean more money is needed in a form that can be used month to month to pay our expenses and, hopefully, to enjoy ourselves in the process. Good planning, at least up to now, has made this possible.

The second retirement issue is tougher. The tools we use to plan for retirement are increasingly unreliable. Pensions, or *defined-benefit* plans, which used to be the standard for retirement in large companies, are often mismanaged and robbed by unethical executives. Though they promise a lifetime of income in retirement, it is doubtful that many of them will be able to pay.

Other retirement plans are managed by us. These are known as *defined-contribution*, and they may meet a similar fate as our monetary system and the stock market become more volatile.

What can you do to protect yourself?

Before we dive into what this book *is*, let's talk about what it is *not*. It is not a get-rich-quick scheme. I will not sugarcoat things, sell you pie-in-the-sky expectations, or tell you that all you have to do is think the right thoughts and success will magically come your way. In short, I want you to know that starting your own business requires a lot of hard work, both physical and mental.

This is also not a book about a particular type of business. I will not be giving you a set of specific tips on how to be a successful grocer, real estate investor or public speaker. I will not give you a step-by-step plan for building a consulting business or selling flowers. Most of all, I will not encourage you to take foolhardy risks by jumping into a business without thoroughly understanding it.

Now for what this book *is*. It is first a book about character. Character is an old-fashioned notion to some people. The cynics of our age have all but chased this word out of our common language. Character is a habit—one that is developed slowly and consistently over a lifetime. Good character comes not just from avoiding doing wrong; it comes from actively pursuing rational values. Character is courage, persistence and independence of thought.

Second, this book is a lesson in learning. No one can possibly teach you how to open a particular business unless you first learn what a business is in general. How you apply these lessons will depend entirely upon your interests, geographic setting, education, skills and motivation. Many times I will refer to the things you need to know outside this book. Successful entrepreneurs learn constantly. They seek new information even when that new information contradicts what they think they already know. Entrepreneurship is not for people who refuse to disturb their warm, comfortable view of the world.

Third, this is a book about action. There is no such thing as an "armchair" entrepreneur. I will be asking you to *do* things as we go along. Some of them will require you to get up out of that comfy chair and hit the street. Think of me as your hired pain-in-the-neck. I promise it will be worth it, even though you may not like it at the time.

Reality-based optimism

I believe that we human beings have a tremendous capacity for not only survival but prosperity. When I say that I am an optimist, I do not mean that I expect events always to unfold as I want them to. When it looks like rain, I carry a raincoat. I do mean that whatever misfortunes arise, we humans are capable of managing them well if we keep our wits about us.

That applies to the present situation. I believe that the answer to the current crisis is learning to rely upon ourselves more. This does not mean you should quit your job. It does mean that you should learn to increase your income through means other than your regular job. This book will show you how or at least get you headed in the right direction.

My beef with most self-help books is that they are written as if the reader were a child. Don't get me wrong; I have benefited tremendously from any number of them over the years. Each has contained at least the seed of a good message. Overall, though, self-help books tend to dazzle the unsuspecting reader with visions of how great life is going to be once he or she starts really "believing." I give you more credit than that.

Let's start with reality. It may sound silly to have to say that, but the past few decades have seen a terrible idea gain ground. It goes by many names, postmodernism and relativism being the most common. The central theme is that there is no such thing as an objective reality. In this view, all of our perceptions, thoughts and opinions are shaped by our culture. Facts are not facts, but rather a particular view of the world shaped by social forces. No particular point of view can make a valid claim to be any better than another. In short, reality is what we wish it to be or what our culture says it is.

Most sane people outside the hallowed halls of our universities recognize this immediately as nonsense. We all know that our upbringing and the culture at large influence many parts of our lives. We also know that some things are true whether we believe them or not. For example, if you have been raised to believe that starting a new business is a noble endeavor (which it is), then you probably will have less trouble taking action than if you believe businesspeople are evil parasites. If you learned early in life that you are capable of learning new things and becoming competent in new skills, you will probably learn new things and become good at them without undue strain. These are examples of how beliefs *do* affect things.

No amount of belief, though, will help you sell a product no one wants or make a bad business model work. Believing will not increase your revenues or reduce your costs—only action will.

Getting started

I am a business professor. I chose this profession because I love the world of business, and I love teaching. Being a professor has given me a rich and rewarding life combining those two loves. Teaching students to expand their thinking and researching ways for people to do business better has made me happier than I ever dreamed possible.

It is in that spirit that I offer you this book. I can show you a few ways to be creative, prepare your business plan and grow your business. I can probably save you some heartache by helping you avoid unnecessary mistakes. If you have the desire to improve your financial life, the courage to learn and the discipline to engage in some hard work, let's get started.

2 Value—the Key to Everything

"Water's precious. Sometimes
may be more precious than gold."

—*Treasure of the Sierra Madre*

 Imagine for a moment a very simple social group. Let's say there are a small band of cave dwellers living by hunting and gathering. Their technology is simple, consisting of rudimentary clothing, bows and arrows for hunting and a simple but serviceable language. One day Og and Ug are talking.

Og: "What wrong you? Look like mastodon poop."

Ug: "Me no sleep good. Freeze all night long."

Og: "Life tough. You no have blanket?"

Ug: "Arrrrggghhhh! Blanket no good. Unravel first week I make!"

Og: "Ouch. And me name Og, not Arrrrggghhhh."

Ug: "You no look so good yourself. What wrong?"

Og: "Me hungry. Miss last five shots. Arrows no fly straight."

Ug: "Hmmmmm... maybe we trade. I make you arrows, and you make me blanket. We trade. Both be better off. Deal?

Og: "Deal."

Congratulations. You just witnessed the first economic transaction. Og and Ug have discovered what was later to become the basis for all civilized societies—trade. The elements of this transaction are simple. Each party receives something useful, something he or she values, in exchange for something he or she has created. Instead of each person making everything himself, individuals find their unique talents and focus on them. Soon Ug the arrow maker and Og the blanket maker become even better at their respective trades and the whole tribe begins to benefit from their expertise.

The key point here is what happens to the whole tribe. Instead of trade being a zero-sum game in which one party gains at another's expense, *both* parties improve their condition. Expand this concept to a whole society, and we see that specialization combined with free trade raises the living standard of all participants. This simple point is lost upon many people, who think that the wealthy benefit only at the expense of the poor. Assuming all transactions are voluntary, no one engages in a trade without first deciding that he or she will be better off afterward.

Let's take our analogy a little further now. What if our imaginary tribe advances to the point where it is cumbersome to barter? For example, perhaps Og needs arrows now, but Ug has no present need for blankets. Instead of barter, they agree to allow Og to give Ug something that signifies the exchange of value. Maybe they use a particular type of shell or tree bark or shiny rocks.

This marks the invention of money. Ug can use his shells, bark, or rocks later to purchase something he needs then. Eventually, people in the tribe who bring more value to others accumulate more money. This is a perfectly natural and just development. No one can fault providers of value for earning more money. In fact, the rest of the tribe should be grateful to have some among them who use their brains to figure out ways to get more value out of the resources they have available.

All businesses, past, present and future, operate on this fundamental principle. If you want more money and are disinclined to steal it or confiscate it through taxation, *you must create value for others.* The remaining chapters of this book explain how to do that, but first let's take a look at more recent developments in our economic system.

The rise of the business organization

Skipping forward a few thousand years we come to the present, where billions of transactions occur hourly. Each one retains elements of that first encounter between Og and Ug. Parties involved in each trade seek to better their situation. As societies grew over the ages, though, isolated exchanges like those described above became impractical. Among other things, markets developed where many people could exchange many things in one place. Information about who has what and who wants what evolved into advertising. Some products needed to be gathered into central distribution centers. Others needed to be spread to remote areas.

About 100 to 150 years ago, truly large organizations emerged to meet the demands of growing markets. Being big was useful because it allowed people to specialize even more. Large companies could take advantage of economies of scale as well, giving us access to products that can only be produced efficiently in large numbers, like cars and computers.

For all their advantages, sizable companies had drawbacks. They tended to be slow to change with the times, and sometimes working for one tended to be stifling for more independent people. The trade-off was that people could get a job instead of having to run their own business. That trend also had a dark side—people became addicted to jobs.

Job addiction

First, let me make it clear that there is nothing wrong with having a job. I have one myself. Having a job is different, though, from creating value on your own and selling it to others. In most cases, a jobholder trades time for money.

Imagine that you hold an hourly wage job. No matter how much value you create for others in an hour, you take home the same amount of money. That seems like a rip-off, but there is a bright side—you take home the same amount of money even if you *don't* create a lot of value. Of course, if you don't create value consistently, you may find yourself without even a job. Why is it to the company's benefit to pay you? They gain more from your production than they pay you, simple as that. It is a great arrangement for both parties as long as the company has a use for you.

What do we give up when we take a job? First, we give up some freedom. We usually have to show up at a certain time, do what our bosses tell us to do and agree to certain other restrictions on our behavior. Second, at least in the case of an hourly wage job, we give up our ability to increase our income through higher production. There are exceptions. Sometimes we get a bonus or a raise, but by and large, we take home the same amount hour after hour, day after day, month after month and year after year.

It is easy for complacency to set in. While a job may become boring or no longer hold a challenge for us, the comfort of knowing that we don't have the hassles of attending to all the million and one details of running a whole business is seductive. We take care of our little corner of the company and let the rest go.

There are some other less obvious downsides to job-holding. As long as you work for someone else, you are making money for him or her. There is nothing wrong with that, but most of us do not think about how *much* money we may be making for someone else. The comfort and predictability of having a job may have a higher price than most of us would care to admit.

Another downside is that you are at the mercy of your employer during downturns such as the current financial crisis. When times get tough, payroll is one of the first cost-reduction targets. Chances are, if you are cut from one company, the demand for whatever it is that you do is down in other companies as well. Getting another job can be tough.

Is the trade-off worth it? Does holding a job even make sense? Only you can answer that question. Your circumstances are unique to you—there is no universal answer for everyone. There are, however, ways to wean yourself from complete dependence on a job.

My lesson in job instability

I am a college professor. If ever there were a stable job, that would be it, or so I thought. In the not-too-distant past, I took a university position with great promise. I was hired to build an entrepreneurship program at a university of about 15,000 students. During my contract negotiations, I agreed to start at a certain base salary, which would be supplemented by a significant amount when the money to support the program was in place. All this was written clearly into my contract and reviewed by my attorney.

A few months after I arrived, the money was given to the university by a donor. In the meantime, a new dean was hired. I patiently waited for my supplemental income. I waited some more. After a time, I spoke to the new dean about this provision, and he informed me that he was not bound by the previous dean's promises. I showed him the contract. He stalled. I waited. You get the picture.

Reluctantly, I hired an attorney and sued. It soon became clear that the university was willing to spend more money winning the lawsuit than it would have just paying me what I was contractually promised. Recognizing I was beat, I settled for a pittance and considered what to do next.

In the end, things worked out. I found a much better position with infinitely more agreeable colleagues. My salary is now much higher than it would have been at the other place.

Something in me changed, though. For one thing, I recognized that my profession does not offer the stability I thought it did. In retrospect, I had done everything anyone could do to ensure that my income was sufficient to make up for moving expenses, a higher cost of living in the new area, and the general disruption of uprooting the family. I had a written agreement, not a verbal promise. I had my attorney look at the agreement. Nothing was left undone, but in the end, one dishonest person was able to drastically disrupt my life.

How could that happen? Moreover, how many other people in professions less stable than mine were subject to the whims of other people in positions of authority? I decided to do two things. First, I immediately made plans to become financially independent. I decided to reach the point where I could walk away from my university job and still be able to live comfortably. Second, I made a vow that I would create my own university, Entrescape. Entrescape (**entrescape.com**) would deliver online education to people like me who recognized that relying solely on a job for income is an invitation to disaster. I wanted to reach potential entrepreneurs willing to escape the tyranny of their jobs.

The entrepreneurial explosion

In some ways, the world has become friendlier to entrepreneurs. In the period from 1980 to 1999, Fortune 500 firms lost more than five million jobs, but more than thirty-four million jobs were created (Reynolds, Hay, and Camp, 1999). During those two decades, we saw the emergence of small business as the real driver of economic progress. Small businesses came to account for more net job creation and more innovation than large companies. The entrepreneurial party had started.

Among the bits of good news was the fact that this revolution was not restricted to any particular group. Women and minorities were among the most enthusiastic participants, starting businesses in droves (Reynolds et al., 1999). Suddenly, new and small were better than old and large.

This trend opened up countless opportunities for the brave and creative. In this span of time, we saw the emergence of the cell phone, the Internet, and wireless connectivity. We saw an unprecedented rise in incomes and an explosion of economic growth. For all the problems we now face, we still have to admit that the last twenty-five years have been good to us.

Creating value your way

All of these trends are important, but they don't really capture the main point. Even starting a business like the ones captured in these statistics can take years. How can people like you and me make money, like, *right now?*

One problem with jobs is that they make us stupid. Even jobs that challenge us in some technical area or that require us to be creative may fail to develop our entrepreneurial skills. It is much like swimming. It's no problem if I don't know how as long as I am on dry land. The moment I fall overboard or slip off the dock, though, there is simply no substitute for being able to swim. If for no other reason than economic survival, it pays to know how to build a business.

Another problem with jobs is that they rarely allow us to do what we really want to do. I am truly blessed in that I do what I love every day. I love teaching, I enjoy doing research and I have a great set of colleagues. What more could a guy want? Well, for me, it is actually *doing* business, not just teaching about it or researching it. Not only does this ensure that my kids won't have to open their guest room for me when I am old; it gets me out doing something I love.

You may love your job, as I do. You may have no desire to quit now or ever. You may even be one of those rare individuals who gets complete fulfillment from a job. If so, stay with what you are doing, by all means. The only thing you need to worry about is job stability and your retirement. Should you lose your job (heaven forfend), this book may come in handy.

This does not describe most people I meet, though. Most people I meet in the halls of my university like what they do. Most are reasonably good at it, too. Even so, they seem half-hearted about their profession. Grinding out papers and teaching yet another class of less-than-motivated students seems more like a drag than a passion. They dread Monday and love Friday. Each week is something to be survived rather than treasured.

I suspect that if I were to hear their innermost thoughts, they would reveal a hidden dream, a nearly smothered passion to do something else. Maybe not instead of, but certainly in addition to, what they already do. So why don't they do it? Why don't *you* do it?

It is because most of us do not have a clue how to take what we love to do and earn money doing it. Say you love drawing. Have you ever tried to sell a drawing? Not easy, huh? Maybe you got some of your work put on the walls of a coffee shop. Maybe you participated in an art show. Those are good efforts. But how many other ways are there to make money drawing? How about selling on the Internet? How about teaching drawing lessons? How about taking commissions for drawings? How about starting a line of greeting cards?

Years ago, there was a popular book suggesting that if you do what you love the money will follow. Not once have I ever had money chase me around. If I were superstitious, in fact, I would believe that it actually runs the other way. Money does not seek us out—we have to seek it out. Seeking out money means that we not only have to create value for others, we also have to make them aware of that value and provide some means for them to get it without too much of a hassle. The next time you hear someone say they tried to earn money _____ ing, but it didn't work, ask them what they did to sell their product or service. Chances are, they made a minimal effort and gave up.

Here is an exercise. Get out a piece of paper or sit down at your computer. I'll wait...

OK. Now, take a couple of deep breaths and relax. This exercise should be fun and stress-free. I want you to list—as rapidly as you can—fifty (yes, fifty) or more things you like to do. Do not criticize or judge anything. Just write (or type). Don't stop until you get fifty. If you like doing somersaults in the front yard on Easter, list that. If you like the feeling you get when you clean the kitchen, list that. If you like doing something that you would never do in public, list it anyway, just don't tell me about it. I don't want to know.

The seven-day business

Hopefully you have a nice collection of ideas ranging from the brilliant to the silly. Be honest with yourself. If you stopped short of fifty, you are not done. Finish what you started and get ready for the next step. First, separate your ideas into two categories: ideas that could be done right away and those that would take a long time. Don't worry too much about getting every idea categorized perfectly. Some will be a judgment call. The important thing is to get every idea into one of the two lists.

Now, forget for a moment about your "dream" business. Just take your list of businesses that could be done right away and look over it. Do some stand out as easier to execute than others? Narrow that list down further to three businesses that you honestly feel you could start today and have at least some revenue in a week. That's right—seven days. It does not matter how much you could sell, just pick a business that stands a good chance of bringing in something in a week.

Do that business—now, not later. Here's how. Get a piece of paper or sit down at the computer. List all the things you need to start. If you need supplies, list them. If you need time, block out your schedule for the next week to include the necessary time. If you need the cooperation of other people, like your spouse, children or friends, make the necessary calls.

Next, find customers. You don't have to contact them yet, just find out who and where they are. For example, if you are going to advise people on how to get rid of clutter, you will write down the names and contact information of people in your circle of neighbors and friends who might need your advice. If you are going to run errands for people, you will do the same. If you are going to sell cookies, you figure out where you could sell them.

Finally, get everything ready to sell. If you are going to make something, make it. If you are going to provide a service, make sure you know what you are going to do. Set your price as best you can to the level you see others charging. If your idea is completely new, do the best you can.

At the end of the week, write down your thoughts about your experience. What was scariest? What was the most fun? What did you do well? What did you do poorly? How much money did you make? Concentrate on the process of opening and running the business. Making money is important, but at this point, I want you to think about the realities of being in business for yourself. Chances are, you found out that it was a mixture of the pleasant and the unpleasant, the easy and the hard, and the simple and the complex.

You may have found something doing the seven-day business that you really love. On the other hand, you may now be eager to try something different. Either way, you know more than you did when you started. Now let's find out how to do a bigger business.

3 Getting Started

"The secret of getting ahead
is getting started."

—*Sally Berger*

 Now you know how to brainstorm business ideas and how to make some money in a short period of time. Keep up the brainstorming habit—it will pay off in spades. It also won't hurt to do a seven-day business now and again just to remind yourself that the possibilities for creating a new business are endless.

What business should I start?

Ideas are terrific things to have. Most people don't have nearly enough. But ideas alone are not worth much. Starting a business requires action, something you discovered in the seven-day business. Starting a business that will provide the extra income and retirement security you want requires several other things. What are they?

First let's explore the difference between an idea and an opportunity. One of my favorite things about being a professor is the refreshing naiveté of my students. Eighteen to twenty-two year-olds still have a view that anything is possible, well, just because. Most of them are also still enthralled with alcohol and the opposite sex. The combination of the two often has hilarious results. Here is an excerpt from a concept statement that was turned in for one of my classes:

> *Club Indigo will be a happening bar within walking distance of campus. It will feature cheap drinks, live bands, and stay open until 3:00am. The theme will be sports. There will be 20 TV sets located throughout the club, all showing your favorite sports all the time. Currently there are no competitors for Club Indigo. All other clubs in the university area charge too much for drinks and never have good service. Our great beer*

*selection and low prices will make us the hottest bar in the
downtown area.*

Aside from an unhealthy fascination with the nightlife, this student has missed some important details. Let's start with customer demand. Here we have a classic case of marketing by personal preference. And if you think this happens only with my undergraduates, think again. I have seen any number of entrepreneurs make the same mistake.

We all tend to think that everyone else thinks like we do. We may say we don't, but we do. I read a lot, and for the life of me, I cannot fathom why everyone else doesn't read all the time. You like to cook, and you cannot imagine someone who eats out all the time. We get ourselves into trouble when we start placing our thoughts in other peoples' heads. My student had over thirty bars to choose from in that college town—you couldn't fit another one in edgewise. But because it was not perfect for him, he thought it was a business opportunity.

Of course, it *might* be an opportunity. If he were to investigate and uncover solid reasons that some niche was not being filled, it may be worth pursuing. The point is that he was thinking about what *he* wanted, not what his customer wanted.

The same concept works in reverse. Sometimes there exist niches that go unexplored. One time I had a member of the community in which I lived approach me with an idea for a way to dispose of cat waste in an ecologically friendly way. I am not fond of cats. For one thing, I am extremely allergic to them. For another, I just plain don't like them (sorry, cat lovers). When I heard the idea, my first reaction was, "Ick." I was also skeptical of the idea itself. It sounded like the bar idea—one that would only appeal to the inventor.

The inventor, Kate, was persistent. She investigated the market, found facts to support her contention that there was a better way, and conducted a focus group to help her refine the idea. She got a provisional patent and constructed a prototype. In the end, I was proven wrong. It was me who had been limiting my thinking.

Another difference between my student and Kate was commitment. My student had a temporary fascination with socializing. Kate had a deep commitment to solve what she perceived as a pressing problem. This is a good lesson for all of us. Lasting businesses are usually started by people who have a deep commitment to something important. It may be as simple as a commitment to provide the best flower shop in your community. You may envision people having someone they can trust to make great recommendations for everything from anniversaries to funerals. You are not selling flowers; you are adding beauty to peoples' lives.

As a practical matter, this translates into finding a market *niche*. Imagine a giant playground where all the favorite spots have the grass worn down. We know from just looking that these are kids' favorite places to play. In fact, if you were a kid and wanted to play there, you probably couldn't—too many people. However, there are plenty of places that are not worn down. Other kids play there, just not as many and not as often. You could have a ball there because you have more room to do what you want to do.

Markets are like that. They have sections (called "market spaces") where the big guys don't play very much. Walmart's gargantuan success revolves around stocking items that "turn" often. That is, the shelf is constantly being restocked. Only certain kinds of items fill the bill. For example, you can bet that everyday household items like towels and washcloths turn over regularly and heavily. But specialty items like high-end dress socks are not generally found there. With the advent of Walmart, specialty retail stores emerged to fill the gaps it could not fill within the confines of its business model.

Your chances of competing with Walmart are slim. The good news is that you don't have to. Instead, find a market space where the big guys don't play and focus, focus, focus.

What do I like to do?

We all have things we like to do. The problem is, "like" can mean a lot of things. I like to watch baseball, but watching it all day long and writing a sports column about it would be boring. I have a friend who likes to record music. He is talented, but he is not interested in promoting his recordings as a business. At least he is not interested enough to really work at it. Sometimes the things we like to do for pleasure become very unpleasant when we try to make a living doing them.

Another problem with "like" is that some activities simply are not salable. For example, I like to watch beautiful sunsets. No one I know is going to pay me to do that. This may sound obvious, but over the years I have met many people who confuse likability with salability. Expecting the money to roll in just because you do what you love is naive.

Another way to think about this is analyzing what you dislike. I have had numerous jobs over the years. I have farmed, sold clothing, sold multi-ply business forms (now there's some real fun) and delivered packages for UPS. Now I am a professor. Each job had its unique appeal, though in a couple of cases it was a strain to find it. After I had experienced enough variety in jobs, I came to a strong conclusion about my dislikes. No matter what the job, I hated punching a clock. I did not mind physical work, like delivering packages. I did not mind selling a boring product all that much (business forms). I really enjoyed selling clothing. Each of these jobs had to be done, though, at a particular time. I had to be "on" whether I felt like it or not.

For me, that meant I had to find a profession where I could pretty much work when I wanted to. I work longer hours now than I ever did in any of my clock-punching jobs. The difference is that I am the one choosing those hours, not someone else. For you, it may be something else. Maybe you hate to work outdoors. Maybe you hate to work indoors. Maybe you hate getting up early. Maybe you hate something else. The point is, find what you hate as well as what you like. And be honest about it.

What am I good at?

We have curious notions about competence in our culture. In some ways, our expectations are way too high. In sports, we tend to take professionals as the standard for performance. Nothing wrong with that, except when we mere mortals compare ourselves to them. The percentage of people who make it to the National Football League or into Major League Baseball, for example, is so low as to be negligible.

You can't enjoy your weekend softball league very much if you constantly compare yourself to Albert Pujols. So "good" is relative.

On the other hand, we tend to be a culture of weenies when it comes to honest feedback about our abilities. In a colossal perversion of the concept of self-esteem, we have come to think of negative feedback as detrimental to the self-esteem of children, workers and spouses. Misspelling has become "creative" spelling. When we don't get a job, we sue. Anything that makes us think we are less than capable becomes suspect.

We all need to grow up.

Being good at something means that you perform at a high level compared to some standard. In business, that standard is always the customer. Love or hate Microsoft, you have to admit that in terms of customers' purchasing patterns, they do well. Being "good" from the point of view of, say, programmers, is only loosely connected to their sales success. Many programmers despise Microsoft products, but it is only now, after twenty-odd years, that there are serious contenders in the marketplace for operating systems. So being "good" for a business means satisfying customers, not whether you or I approve.

Witness entertainers. We have all endured public performances where a person's own opinions of their talent outstripped their real talent. Those folks need a good friend to tell them the truth, but few of us are willing to be that kind of friend. In the marketplace, people are not reluctant to tell us whether we have done well or not. They do not have to take us aside, buy us a cup of coffee and then hem and haw as they explain to us why we are not as talented as we think. They simply don't buy what we have to offer.

So how do you decide what you are good at? Things you have excelled at in the past are a good start. Take an inventory of skills and knowledge you have developed over the years. Don't overlook skills that you do not immediately recognize as salable. Include also things you have done as a volunteer. For example, are you active in church and social groups? Do you organize events regularly? Have you helped raise money?

Somewhere in the interplay of what you like to do and what you are good at is the seed of a business idea. Dig deep—the most obvious ideas may not be the best ones.

Sometimes a skill set needs to be complemented. When I was in my early twenties, I studied martial arts with friend of mine named Sam. He earned his black belt a few months before I did and was already teaching quite a bit in the school. Sam was a talented martial artist and soon after our instructor left the area, he opened his own school.

The trouble was, Sam loved to train more than he loved to promote the school. For a while, that led to problems with revenues. His father-in-law, a sales professional, taught him to do the necessary work of making phone calls and selling memberships before he trained each afternoon. Before long, he had a steady flow of students and became one of the most recognized and respected schools in the area. Thirty years later, he is still open. Sam, like many of us, liked doing something but had to learn how to make the business part of it work.

Why would anyone pay for what I have to offer?

Software astounds me. Everything that happens in a computer is, on the most basic level, a zero or a one—it is all based on a binary system. Every time I think of the billions and billions of zeros and ones it takes to do the simplest computer task, my mind shorts out. Yet we use this wonderful stuff daily.

Early in the history of consumer software, a battle raged over property rights. Could someone own the rights to a piece of software? In other words, if I wrote a program, could I then sell it and prevent others from copying it without paying? In the end, of course, property rights were established for software. In my view, this made perfect sense. Like a novel, I own it if I create it.

Though there are many sides to the argument, one benefit of paying for software was that a lot of it got developed in a short time. The competition for operating systems, for example, led to the establishment of Microsoft as the dominant company providing operating systems as well as other commonly used software.

Recently, things have changed. Now open source software is emerging as a viable alternative to paid software. Open source is free, put together by teams of volunteers. I predict that the days when anyone pays for software are numbered.

How can this be? Since this is not a treatise on the economics of property rights, let me just say that people have discovered that there is a bundle of money to be made supporting software even if the software itself is free. It's kind of like getting a cell phone for next to nothing. The phone seller knows that money can be made from monthly fees. Or, it's like giving away a printer knowing that you will sell a heck of a lot of printer cartridges in the future. The point is, you may have become rich twenty years ago writing software, but you are unlikely to pull that one off now. People are changing their perceptions.

Whether people will pay for something is often not obvious. Personal trainers come to mind. At one time, people may have had workout partners, but only Olympians had coaches or personal trainers— maybe a few celebrities. Conversely, more people had personal servants or housekeepers a hundred years ago than now. As times change, so do people's perceptions of value.

So how do you find out whether people will buy what you have to offer? An MBA student will tell you to start with market studies, conduct focus groups, and launch an awareness campaign. All of that is fine if you happen to have a $50 million advertising budget. I don't have one. Do you?

The right answer is to get out there and sell something. Take reasonable precautions to follow the law. For example, don't try to sell home-brewed beer on the street corner or rent people out for, ahem, companionship. But get out there and sell something. If you make sales, it is a good indication that your product or service has legs. If not, you may need to think through your offering and revise it or abandon it. Either way, it is better to know that before you spend a lot of money on expensive advertising.

One of the best examples I ever saw was a group of students in one of my entrepreneurship classes. The team leader had a hobby of cooking up beef jerky. He had learned to make a tender, flavorful version that his friends loved. I encouraged them to try selling a batch to other consumers. They checked out university regulations, found out they could sell on campus with certain restrictions and opened up shop one horribly rainy Thursday. Within forty-five minutes, they were sold out. As I write this book, they have taken the next step toward growing a real business. No amount of market research, valuable as it is, can substitute for that kind of hands-on testing.

Full- or part-time?

There is a persistent myth about entrepreneurship that goes something like this. The only successful entrepreneurs are those who throw caution to the wind, risk everything, quit their jobs and put themselves in a situation in which they have to make it.

Not quite.

Evidence compiled by Amar Bhide (2000) shows that, in fact, many new businesses that go on to be successful are started part-time. Many times, entrepreneurs hold regular jobs until the time they either no longer want or no longer need to have a job. Sometimes, they just continue to do the business part-time.

What is right for you? Well, that depends. There are two major factors in deciding whether you are better off part- or full-time. First, there is the practical matter of how much time you have. Someone with a regular forty-hour a week job has to work around the time scheduled for that. A retired person with little to do has more options. A stay-at-home mom or dad may be somewhere in between.

Second, there is the psychological component. Let's look at that one more closely. Commitment is a necessity for any entrepreneurial business. We human beings have a funny notion of time. In the comfort of the living room, it is easy to say that you will devote your nights and weekends to your new business. When it actually comes time to do that, though, time may be scarcer than you think. If you are accustomed to working regular hours, it may be difficult to discipline yourself to work when you don't have to.

The best way to find out if you are cut out for this kind of commitment is to make a safe foray into your new schedule. Try this. Research your best business idea during the hours you would normally work your new business. Don't worry, we'll cover business plan writing in a later chapter. Discipline yourself to spend certain hours working and see how it goes. How you do at this experiment will give you great insight into whether you can stick to it when you actually open for business.

Another factor to consider is your purpose. Some people just want to supplement their income. I suggest you be more specific. At the outset of this book, I cautioned you that we are headed for a gigantic mess economically. Please don't start a great business and then fritter away your money on toys, leaving you right back where you started. Secure your retirement first, and then buy some toys.

Other people want to grow themselves out of their current jobs. This can be a great goal if it is done right. "Doubling up" may be a strain in the short run, but in the long run, it is a good sign when you realize you do not have to have a job anymore. It also gives you some flexibility in how you make the transition to self-employment and a steadier cash flow in the meantime.

What if I don't have any spare cash?

Though this may sound strange, lack of cash is usually the least of your worries. I am not saying it is not a challenge—it is. But on the list of things you will have to deal with, getting cash will be further down than you think. Let's talk about some ways to get what you need without being flush with cash.

First, figure out how much cash you do have. Count CDs, savings accounts and other money squirreled away somewhere. For right now, let's not count your retirement accounts. Add all that up. Is it more than zero? You have enough money, then. If it is literally zero, that's OK too. If you had all the money you needed, you wouldn't be thinking about earning more, right?

Now, ask yourself how much of that you would be willing to risk. In other words, how would things look if you were to lose all of what you use for your new business? Expect the worst-case scenario to be bad. That's why it is called "worst-case." If you can live with the worst case, you will probably find the risk worth it.

The figure you come up with may be $10 or $10,000. It does not matter at this point. I want you to think of that as your seed money—money that will be used to grow your business. Are we all done? Good. Now forget about cash. Lack of cash is an excuse. In fact, it is probably the most used excuse of all time for not starting a business. Think of it this way. A man needs new shoes. His friend asks him why he doesn't go get some. "What? Walk to the shoe store in these worn-out shoes?"

You can't get started on a journey with everything you will possibly need at your disposal, cash included. In addition to being a convenient excuse, lack of cash is a mentality that blocks us from seeing other resources. What is important is not the money you have, but the resources you control. Do you own a computer? Well, there is one heck of a resource. You don't have to buy it—you already have it. How about a skill? There's another one. And what about your friends? Do they have resources? Maybe it's money, or maybe it's knowledge or skills or something else.

Aside from friends and family, there are loads of other places to find resources. Clever entrepreneurs often find suppliers who are willing to extend credit or money partners who are willing to count your "sweat equity." Remember, you don't have to own resources—you just have to control them.

Developing a business model

A business model is a simple, clear, and concise way of describing what you do. Just as a model airplane leaves out the details of its larger counterpart, so a business model gets right to the core of what a business does. If you make decorative baskets, you take raw material like baskets and stuff to go in them, you arrange this "stuff" and you sell the baskets. Pretty simple. If you have a web site on gardening tips, you may sell memberships to people who want to receive information and network with others who garden.

Developing a business model requires that you streamline and clarify your thinking. It is shocking to me to go to venture capital conferences only to hear entrepreneurs talk endlessly about their product. Investors start fidgeting after about three minutes of that. They want to know what makes the business tick, not the product. The product is not the business model. Let's go back to our gardening web site example. Say instead of having people pay for memberships, you sell advertising on the site. These are two different business models, each requiring different strategies and approaches.

The key concept of a business model is how you actually add value to something. Value-added has unfortunately become a business school buzzword, rendering it virtually devoid of meaning. Nonetheless, the idea behind it is valid. In order to sell something, you have to add value to something. Take the example of a house. Though house flipping has become an unattractive business because of the housing meltdown, it still makes a good example of how to add value to something.

The first time I heard of house flipping, I laughed. A couple I knew claimed to be doing well by taking unattractive but not completely run-down houses, cleaning them up a bit, and reselling them. Being the curious and skeptical type, I asked for some details. What they told me changed my opinion completely. By just cleaning up the landscaping and painting, they were able to increase the market value of homes by as much as $20,000. Their cost was trivial compared to the increase in value, and this was in a market that was only appreciating at 3% a year.

Here is the lesson. The value you add to something, be it a house or anything else, must be more than your cost of making it more valuable. You can't know whether that is true until you sketch out a business model. Doing so is as simple as answering these three questions:

1. How do I get something that can be made more valuable?
2. How do I make it more valuable?
3. How do I get my money after making it more valuable?

The first question is subtler than it first appears. Web site business owners are notorious for being confused about what they do. I have seen interminable investor presentations for web sites where the founders of a web business are unable to explain exactly what they do. The fact that thousands or even millions of people visit a web site is no guarantee that it makes money. Do you provide content? Then you have to have something new and valuable on that site for people to see. Do you work behind the scenes, making web sites better? Fine, but you need to know that up front.

Second, how do you actually do what you do? A massage therapist may work in a medical clinic, a massage business, a spa or out of his or her home. A teacher may give live workshops or webinars. A farmer may own land or lease it. A landowner may farm himself or lease out the land. For every general category of business, there are dozens of ways to deliver the goods (add value).

Third, take the example of flipping houses. One way to earn money is to fix up houses and get paid for doing so. Or, you might work for a real estate investor who flips houses or someone who rents them out or a homeowner who just wants to spruce things up. In that case, your value added is still the fixing up, but the way you get paid is different. Hence, a different business model—the owner pays you. If you were flipping the house yourself, the buyer of the spruced up house would be the source of your income.

Identifying markets

Value is in the eye of the beholder. Unless you are selling one great big thing, like the Louisiana Purchase, you will need to identify lots of people who value your product or service. There are only two kinds of value: things people realize they need, and things people need, but do not yet realize they need.

How can anyone need something they don't know about? Who needed a home computer thirty years ago? We all made it just fine without one. It took Steve Jobs and Bill Gates to teach us how valuable they were. Now we would not dream of being without one, maybe several. The same goes with safety razors. King Gillette improved on the barbaric process of dragging an open blade across one's throat every morning.

You may have something that few people know they need. In that case, you have to create the new product, and make people aware of how much they need it. That can be a tall order for a small new company. Normally, a small new company should focus on a market that already exists. Better yet, it should focus on a product or service that has a new twist on an old idea (Bhide, 2000). The market may exist, but the niche you pick represents a new feature, a new delivery system, or a new set of customers.

How do you find these markets? First, just ask. If possible, create some products or offer some services to people who can be reached easily. That may include friends, colleagues, and family. If your grandmother won't buy one, maybe you should reconsider your idea. Next, get data from the Internet. Is this a well-defined market? Does it show growth trends or stagnation and decline trends? Is it an old market (shoes) or a new one (cell phone covers). Does it depend on other markets? (It is hard to sell phone covers if no one uses phones anymore.)

While the Internet is handy, it is limited in some ways. Also go to trade journals and popular magazines. Books are great. Best of all, find a mentor—someone who can help you avoid some of the mistakes they made. By gathering information from all these sources, you will become better informed and armed against avoidable mistakes.

4 Financial Projections for the Accounting-Impaired

"There's no business like show business, but there are several businesses like accounting."
—David Letterman

 And now for a subject that sends some people under the table to cry like a little kid— spreadsheets. Not to worry, I will make this painless. In fact, at the end of this chapter, you will have a new appreciation for why we do things the way we do when we track our finances and when we make financial projections.

First, let's get one thing straight. You are not training to be an accountant. If you are, you probably don't need this chapter. Or maybe you do. I have met any number of accountants who could get everything on the right line but still could not use that information to make good business decisions. Your goal is simple—you want to be able to understand how money works in your business and how to ask intelligent questions of the person you hire to keep your books. That's right, as soon as it is feasible, you will want to hire someone else to do your accounting for you.

Accounting is a noble profession. The people who are good at it are invaluable to you. Just remember that, like lawyers, they are your advisors. They do not run your business. You do. For our purposes, we want to understand the flow of cash more than anything else. When we get to the income statement, we run into ways of dealing with money that help us manage our business but are well beyond the scope of this book—likewise for the balance sheet. All three major financial statements are essential to a full understanding of finance, but for new businesses, the cash flow statement rules.

The reason is simple. New businesses are usually cash-starved. You want to know your cash position and cash trends well before any disasters appear. An income statement may show your business as being profitable right up until the time your utilities are shut off.

The historical cash flow statement

The super-accountant way to generate a cash flow statement is to start with the income statement and the balance sheet and work to the middle. In other words, they generate it last. Before you go telling your accountant that he or she is crazy for doing that, let me explain why it is done that way.

Often, income taxes are based on the income statement, loosely speaking. Since the income statement accounts for some things differently than a cash flow statement does, the taxes you owe when you start making money cannot be accurately figured from the cash flow statement. This presents a conundrum. We cannot easily link our tax return to our cash flow statement.

For *historical* statements, this is not a problem. We already know how much we *actually* paid in taxes in the past. When we get to *pro forma* statements, it is a different matter. Pro forma statements are *pro*-jections into the future. Accurately guessing cash flows into the future requires knowing upcoming tax bills. For the moment, let's put that issue aside and focus on a simple way to keep track of cash in your business.

The method I teach was developed over the course of several years. I became frustrated with my students' inability to do basic accounting, even though each was required to have two accounting courses before they took my class. My problem was twofold. First, there were students who knew nothing about accounting. These were the ones who cleared out their memories at the end of those two semesters. Common accounting phrases meant nothing to them. On the other end of the spectrum were those who knew, or thought they knew, a lot about accounting.

For the know-nothing group, I could not re-teach accounting. For the other group, I constantly got esoteric questions about where some obscure item should go on the income statement or the balance sheet. Both groups had the same root problem—they were thinking like accountants rather than entrepreneurs. The know-nothings were scared to death they would get something on the "wrong" line, while the accounting whiz kids were so wrapped up in getting stuff on the "right" line that they missed the point—understanding how money works in a business.

One blessed day I threw away the accounting book. I literally sat down at my computer, opened up a spreadsheet program, and asked myself a simple question. If I did not know anything at all about accounting, how would I track money in a business? After some thought, I realized that I should start with accounting for cash. A little more thought and I developed a simple method for tracking cash that would help my students understand the flow of money in a business. It requires only four major concepts. Let's look at a home-based basket-making business.

Say our basket maker is named Betty. Betty the basket maker makes baskets at home, at least for now. She has dedicated half of her basement to her business. She started by making a few baskets for friends and relatives, who encouraged her to start selling them. She did, and now sells about twenty baskets a month for $40 each. Betty has decided to open a separate checking account and to write a plan for her first "real" year in business.

She starts by estimating how many baskets she can sell in the next twelve months. To make things simple, let's assume a business has only one checking account and that all transactions are by check. No matter what kind of business it is, there are only two things that can happen in that account. Money either comes in or it goes out. Thus the first two concepts: cash in and cash out. The *cash in* category contains all money that comes into the account from any source. At this point, we do not care whether it came from sales or from money you put into the account to get the business started, or interest on your checking account. Everything that comes in goes into the cash in category. All expenditures, no matter what they are for, go in the cash out category.

So far, so good. Now we have something to work with. All we need to do is take the checkbook register and put every transaction into one of those two categories. Everything derives from a check that was written or a deposit slip that was generated when money went into the account; nothing else matters. Here is a sample list of items that might go in the cash in column in January, her first month in business.

$500   Betty's investment into the business
+ $400   Basket sales
_____
$900   **Total cash in for January**

Now let's look at a list of typical expenses.

$	50	Office supplies
+ $	100	Material for baskets
+ $	50	Packaging material
$	200	Total cash out for January

At this point, every cash transaction is accounted for in one of two categories. Neat, huh? The problem is, there is still not much we can do with this information to help us run this basket business. For that, we need two more categories: *cash flow* and *cash balance.* Cash flow is simply *cash in* minus *cash out*:

$	900	Total cash in
- $	200	Total cash out
$	700	Positive cash flow

That means Betty has a positive cash flow of $700 for January. This number could have been negative had she spent more than she brought in. If this is her first month in business, her cash flow for the entire month equals her cash balance at the end of the month, or $700.

February's cash in looks like this:

$	480	Basket sales (12 baskets @ $40 ea.)
$	480	Total cash in for February

Now for cash out:

$	125	Material for baskets
+ $	50	Packaging material
$	175	**Total cash out for February**

Total cash flow for the business is calculated exactly the same way.

$	480	Cash in
- $	175	Cash out
$	305	**Cash flow**

But wait. We almost forgot something. Betty had a cash balance of $700 at the end of January. We need to add that to her February numbers to get an accurate cash balance.

$	700	Cash balance at end of January
+ $	305	Cash flow during February
$	1005	**Cash balance at end of February**

There, that's all you need. Well, almost. I encourage you to start using this method to track your personal finances if you don't already. After you are comfortable with that, start studying some basic accounting. Simply knowing your cash flow and cash balance month-to-month enables you to make better decisions. Knowing how an accountant looks at numbers will help even more. Now, what about planning for your new business?

The pro forma cash flow statement

Since a pro forma statement of any kind is a guess, it is incomplete without an explanation of how the numbers were derived. Think of it as a story that is based on fact. You know, the "based on a true story" type of thing you see on TV. The closer your story is to reality, the more believable it is. If we see a movie about someone who is abducted by aliens, given the secret to eternal life by one of Elvis's clones aboard the spaceship, and sent back to Earth to spread the word, most of us would be, well, dubious. If we see a movie about someone who is lost in the mountains for three months and survives by building a shelter and fighting off wild animals with a stick, we might find it unusual but at least believable.

It is the same with a business plan, the core component of which is a pro forma financial statement. The more I can base my "story" on fact, the more likely people will be to invest in the business or support me in other ways. The more it sounds like fantasy, the less enthused they will be. The trick is to weave facts and guesswork together seamlessly. There is a bit of an art to this, but most of us can do a passable job right from the start.

For the sake of simplicity, let's say this is the end of February. Betty sold ten baskets in January without really advertising. In February, she sold twelve baskets. She estimates that by getting a web site and doing a little promotion at local farmers markets and home shows she can increase her basket sales by two baskets a month every month. A little math shows us that she will sell forty-two baskets a month by December. Not bad.

Why only two baskets a month? Why not five, or ten, or zero? The truth is, there is no *right* estimate—only a more believable or less believable one. Zero may be a good estimate if Betty has no desire to build the business. We are assuming she does. On the other hand, an increase of ten a month would result in 130 baskets a month by December. This *could* happen, but Betty does not think she can reach that level without traditional advertising. At this point, she thinks this is prohibitively expensive. Furthermore, she would have to hire at least two assistants, which would increase her expenses even more.

Favoring the one-step-at-a-time approach, Betty has opted to go for an increase of two baskets a month. Other people may be more aggressive, but for the present, she is fine with this revenue projection.

Now for her expenses. Since she keeps good records, Betty knows that every basket she sells for $40 costs her $10 in raw material. In other words, she makes a $30 *gross margin*. This is a good number to know. In accounting, the cost of raw materials is known as Cost of Goods Sold, or COGS. It means that she effectively has $30 to pay for other expenses for every basket she sells. Whatever is left over is hers to keep. (Note: This calculation of COGS is not the one normally used by accountants. They "tie" these direct expenses to a unit of sales by tracking inventory.)

What are those "other" expenses? First, Betty has to pay for some office supplies. They include paper, stamps, envelopes—that kind of thing. She uses them to send thank-you notes to customers and to contact referrals. They cost $50 a month. The difference between this kind of expense and COGS is that it cannot be linked directly to a particular basket. For example, Betty might send three referral letters to the friends of Sid, who bought a basket yesterday, but only one to friends of Shirley, who bought one the same day. She *could* track that, but it's not worth the trouble. Instead, she lumps all her office supplies into one category.

Some expenses could be treated either way. Packaging material will run roughly the same for each basket. Again, though, it is probably not worth figuring that out. Betty can lump all these together as well. Taken together, all the expenses that are *not* COGS are called *administrative expenses.* Sometimes you will hear them called "overhead."

Dividing expenses into these two categories gives us some helpful information. As I noted above, Betty knows that for every basket she sells, she makes $30. Out of that, she pays her other expenses. Since her other expenses add up to $100 ($50 in office expenses and $50 in packaging material), she has to sell a little over three baskets to break even (cover all her expenses, both COGS and administrative).

Now for the rest of the story. If Betty were to carry out this kind of thinking for the rest of the year, she would end up with an estimate of how much money she would make by December 31. If she were to write out a brief explanation of her figures and how she got them, describe how she was going to reach customers, and tell how she would actually make the baskets, she would have a nice start on writing a full business plan.

Using the pro forma to plan

All these numbers are nice, but what good do they do us? Specifically, what good does it do Betty to guess what will happen in the future? Why not just wait until it happens, since no one can predict the future?

That is a good question, and I am glad you asked. No one can predict *for sure* how Betty's business will do. However, there are strong guesses and weak guesses. Think of it like this. Any baseball team can, theoretically, beat any other team on any given day. That is part of what makes the game of baseball so interesting. But the chances of a struggling team plagued with injuries beating a healthy team with a sterling record are slim. If two people were to predict the winner of a match between the two, one of whom is a baseball enthusiast and the other who knows absolutely nothing, we figure the enthusiast has a better chance of being right. This is so because he or she knows all the factors like injuries that contribute to a win. Our enthusiast could be wrong, but given several sets of predictions like this, we would bet on him or her to be right more often.

The same goes with Betty. If she reasons things through as she did above, she can make a reasonable guess as to her income and her expenses. If she were to just guess without relying on any data (as most small business owners do), we would have no confidence in her predictions. Since she has reasoned her projections through, she has the power to avoid, not all mistakes, but at least the dumb ones.

If Betty is in the ballpark with her predictions, there are several handy things she can figure out. The first is whether she *can* make money. A good place to start is comparing her COGS to her selling price.

If it costs her more to make a basket than she can get by selling it, she need go no further—she cannot make money. An old joke tells of a business owner trying to convince an investor to buy part of his business. The investor looks at his numbers and says, "It costs more to make one of these widgets than you can sell it for." The nonplussed entrepreneur replies, "Yes, we lose money on every unit, but we'll make it up in volume!"

We know that Betty passes the first test. She makes $30 on each basket. We also know that she can cover her other costs by selling a little over three baskets a month. That is good news. Given her sales history, she has every reason to believe that she can sell more than three a month. Had either one of these simple calculations resulted in a negative number, she could have stopped right there. Betty could continue to make baskets because she enjoys it, though she won't make any money. But we have forgotten something important—Betty's time.

The time factor

It would be helpful to calculate how well her time is being spent. If it takes her an hour to make a basket, she makes $30 an hour. If it takes her ten hours, she makes $3 an hour. Big difference. It does not really matter whether Betty *actually* pays herself. She may choose to leave that money in the business to fund future growth. She may not need it for living expenses. Either way, it is good to know how well she spends her time.

The hard part is being honest with yourself about the time actually spent on a business. In Betty's case, it is easy to piddle here and there on baskets and not really count that time. Not that there is anything wrong with working piecemeal like that, it's just that if she does not count that time, she misleads herself about her cost per basket.

Aside from the little bits of time here and there unaccounted for, there are the supplementary things that should count, but often are not. For example, trips to the store for materials or time spent paying bills are easy to overlook. In Betty's case, she may do other things at the same time, like getting groceries. Some judgment is required here, but you see the point—not counting one's time is a mistake.

What can we do after we know how much time we spend on our business? Two things stand out. First, we can figure out if our business is worth it. If it only makes us $2 an hour after some honest calculations, we don't have a business—we have a hobby. Second, it gives us the ability to set some reasonable goals for increasing our income. If Betty works full time, she realistically only has so many hours left to make baskets. If she does not work at all, she has much more flexibility.

As you ponder starting a business, conduct an honest assessment of how much you want to increase your income. Take that amount per year and divide it by the number of hours you are willing and able to work on your business. Next, figure out how much money you can make doing that particular business. There should be a rough match between the two. If there is not, you may need to rethink doing that particular business.

Now let's take a look at some of the psychological factors in opening your own business. Let's talk about character.

5 Why Character Counts

"Happiness is the meaning and the purpose of life, the whole aim and end of human existence."

—*Aristotle*

For at least two thousand years, and probably well before that, thoughtful people have pondered what it means to be happy. Aristotle, certainly one of history's most thoughtful people, called it the ultimate aim in life. Every other desirable thing, according to him, is pursued because it leads to something else (Adler, 1978:93). Money, for example, is pursued not because having money is an end in itself, but because having money allows us to acquire the things that make us happy. Likewise, we enjoy friendship, good food, good books and any number of other things because they make us happy. When it comes to happiness itself, though, we have reached the end of the line. We do not seek happiness for the sake of anything else—we pursue it because that is the point of life.

The word "happiness" may be a poor translation. Scholars often prefer the translation "flourishing life." This may sound like nitpicking, but it is not. Happiness to some people suggests passive enjoyment— pleasure, if you will. A flourishing life, on the other hand, is active.

It is easy to see why passive pleasure, while valuable in its own right, has its limits. Imagine a life in which your every wish were granted instantly. It sounds fantastic, and after a day of life's usual aggravations, I have to admit that fantasy has its appeal. But keep fantasizing. You want something to eat, there it is. Thirsty? Whatever you want, instantly. Sex, money, entertainment, everything—all there whenever you desire it. I sometimes have my students close their eyes for a few minutes and see how long they can last without getting dreadfully bored. Many joke, of course, that this sounds like their idea of heaven. In the end, though, most realize that endless passive pleasure is not what human beings are designed for.

Instead, we are wired for achievement. Merely staying alive requires effort, and millions of years of evolution rewarded those of our ancestors who were good at making the right kind of effort. We forget that fact these days, as most of us live in situations where daily survival is not seriously in question. When it is not necessary to employ all of our efforts in surviving, we *invent* ways to strive against obstacles. Sports are a terrific example.

Paradoxically, we cannot live fully without challenges. We *think* what we want in life is easy access to pleasure. What we *really* want is to be engaged in activities that make us feel alive. Research by Csíkszentmihályi demonstrates that most people are happiest when in *flow* (Csíkszentmihályi, 1990). Flow is that feeling we get when striving for something that is challenging but attainable for us. We tend to forget ourselves and lose track of time, among other things. Unfortunately, our jobs fail to give us this kind of feeling very often, if at all.

According to Victor Frankl, a psychiatrist and survivor of the Nazi concentration camps, it is *meaning* we are after (Frankl, 1988). Meaning to Frankl is not an abstract notion. One's life does not "mean" something outside the context of action. Meaning is the pursuit, the active pursuit, of values that ignite the spark of significance in each of us. It differs for each of us, and each must find his or her own particular way of experiencing it. Of the things that kept people from giving up completely in those horrid conditions, one of the most important was having something to do after imprisonment. The dream of writing a book, returning to a loved one, or achieving something important kept people alive under conditions most of us can scarcely imagine. Those who lost hope about the future soon curled up and died.

What does that have to do with starting a business? To start with, it helps us make sense of the fact that new ventures are hard. We have to confront not only the inevitable problems of doing business, but we have the flexibility to design our business so that it is meaningful to us. This is both a blessing and a curse. Our jobs, with some exceptions, are designed by someone else. We fit ourselves into our work rather than designing our work to fit us. If the fit works out, fine. We are happy, or at least content.

In starting a new business, though, it is not enough to be content. It requires every ounce of our resolve to see through the task of creation. As we will see in a moment, opening a new business also brings us face-to-face with ethics.

Why be good?

Amid all of the hullabaloo over corporate ethics in recent years, it is easy to lose the main point. We see headlines describing the ethical lapses of the highest officers in some of our nation's largest companies and wonder how it could happen. We find ourselves baffled by a system that allows a few unscrupulous predators to bankrupt the retirement funds of thousands of employees. What kind of values (or lack of values) could prompt that kind of behavior?

The basic problem, in my view, is the underlying premise that doing wrong would be good if only we could get away with it. In other words, the reasons offered for being good are *external* restraints.

Some people, sociopaths among them, need others to force them to be good. In extreme cases (think Ted Bundy), they have to be locked up or executed to keep them from harming others. But in the final analysis, being good because someone else will punish you seems shallow and childish.

The real reason to be good is self-interest. Forget for a moment headline-grabbing types of ethical lapses and think about your starting a business. Chances are, you will be dealing with customers, suppliers, and other folks who know you. How long do you think you will get customers if you cheat them? What if you don't exactly cheat them but simply deliver sub-par service? Is that a form of cheating? Not paying your bills on time? How long will suppliers work with you?

But again, these are, in a sense, external restraints. The assumption is that bad things will happen to you if you are not good. I think the real reason to be good is simple self-respect. My father was a good man. His greatest source of pride was his integrity, a trait he worked hard to pass down to my brother and me. Dad used to say to me, "Son, if you can look yourself in the mirror every morning and like what you see, everything else will take care of itself." I have always worked to live up to that ideal, but it took me years to understand the real message behind it. The world is an unstable place. People change, institutions grow and perish, and cultural norms drift. One thing does not change, though, and that is the fact that the person you look at every morning in the mirror will still be there tomorrow.

Dad's litmus test was harsher than any threat of jail or a fine could be. To me, having done wrong was a terrible burden even if no one would ever find out what I did. There was a time in my life during which

I was broke, depressed, drinking heavily, and running around with the wrong group of people. Though I did the right thing numerous times when I could have done otherwise, there were some lapses. Most of them were minor, but they still bothered me. Some could not be helped. When my first business closed, some people lost their membership money. That bothered me, but what bothered me the most was being unable to pay one of my employees her last paycheck.

Could I have paid her? Maybe. The truth is I needed a few hundred dollars to move. I had nothing—absolutely nothing. Without that money, I could not hope to recover. So I kept it, used it to move to Florida, and set about rebuilding my life. Exactly one year later, I called my former employee. I had saved her phone number for the express purpose of this call. She answered the phone, and I said, "Joy, this is Terry Noel. Don't hang up—I want to send you some money." After a moment of silence, she said, "I never expected to get this. Thanks."

Now, let's keep in mind that I was still not flush with cash. I could have used that money for plenty of things besides paying back an employee who had given up hope of ever getting paid. But the feeling I had when I hung up the phone was a thousand times better than the feeling I would have gotten from spending that money. In one brief moment, everything Dad had taught me about self-respect came home, and I realized that the best reason to be good has nothing to do with rules or the law. It has everything to do with that person in the mirror.

Positive virtue

Another beef I have with popular treatments of ethics is the focus on avoiding doing badly to the exclusion of actively doing good. The virtues required of an entrepreneur are more than being honest and delivering what you promise. They also include positive virtues like persistence, courage and independence of thought. This is not for the faint of heart.

Let's tackle persistence first. There is a difference between persistence and stupidity. Persistence is the willingness to try over and over in the face of obstacles. Stupidity is doing it the same way. It never ceases to amaze me how people repeatedly walk into brick walls without stopping to think that they could simply go around it. Of course, I am as guilty as anyone on this count. Farming taught me persistence, but it came with a healthy dose of stupidity. When all you think about is finishing plowing the field, you tend to get locked into one way of doing it.

But what does it mean to be persistent without being dumb? Therein is the real problem. Changing strategies is the most obvious way. Even the big guys do this. Bill Gates for some time considered the Internet a fad with little practical value. Once he realized that the Internet held virtually unlimited business potential, he changed Microsoft's focus and never looked back. Doing so required a type of humility many entrepreneurs lose after their initial successes.

In my own case, I wanted to earn money by teaching martial arts. Owning my own school had proved to be a disaster. Despite my best efforts, I lost everything. A few months later I was making money hand over fist. The difference? I kept my eyes open for an opportunity. When I moved to Florida and found a job selling health club memberships, times were tough. I was working commission-only sales, and my clientele had not yet built up. One day as I walked by our new aerobics room, I realized no one used it after eight thirty. I asked the club manager if I could use it to teach karate at that time. He said yes, and that he would not even charge me for the space.

Without overhead, I was able to make plenty of money with little investment. At that time, the early nineteen eighties, virtually all martial arts schools were housed in strip malls or freestanding buildings. That meant they were paying rent for a facility that could only generate income for a few hours at night. I had inadvertently discovered a trend. Soon, most schools were located in health clubs for the same reason I had done so—low overhead.

The lesson I learned is that I did not have to give up my original idea. I loved teaching karate, and I wanted to make money at it. Having my own exclusive space only *seemed* like a part of the plan. I had lower expenses and fewer headaches by using a resource rather than owning or renting it.

This willingness to change course has come in handy over the years. How do you know when to quit altogether? That all depends on how important your original goal is and what parts of that goal are essential. In the case of martial arts for me, making money was critical, and I wanted to do it by teaching. Other goals of mine proved to be unattainable or undesirable.

For example, one time I bought into a multi-level sales company of health products. I anted up for a good amount of inventory and found that pushing vitamins was extremely distasteful. For one thing, I was living in a small apartment at the time, and it was difficult to hold meetings there. For another, some of the claims of the company I represented were dubious. Being a rational person, I questioned whether all of these products were necessary for general health, and I knew for sure that some claims were outright false. It is hard to put your heart into something you don't really believe in, so I pulled the ripcord and closed the business.

Few highly successful businesses retain their original business model. As they grow, the founders usually learn that there are better ways to do things. Penicillin was discovered when Fleming noticed a stray mold was killing bacteria. He was not looking for it. Post-it notes were the result of research on a super-strong adhesive formula that did not work. The microwave oven was discovered when a research scientist walked by a radar tube and the chocolate bar in his pocket melted. None of these ideas would have succeeded had the originators stuck with their original plans or been blind to new insights.

The second positive virtue is courage. Courage is not rashness or foolhardiness. It is the ability to act even in the presence of fear. Someone who has no fear is not in his or her right mind. Fear is a perfectly natural reaction to a set of circumstances that is perceived as threatening. Notice I said *perceived* as threatening. Events themselves are not seen the same by everyone. Some people (like me) *love* to speak in public. Others are terrified.

Years ago, I earned my private pilot license. Most people do not realize that rental airplanes are essentially tin cans with wings. Since they are used by scores of different people, things get worn and loose. To the pilot, this is not a problem as long as the wings stay on and the engine runs. To an inexperienced passenger, this can be unnerving. When I took my wife for her first flight in a small plane with me as a pilot, my door came open on final approach. I calmly slammed it shut and continued to set up my approach. Briefly, out of the corner of my eye, I saw my wife frozen in horror, unable to speak. When we landed and I shut down the engine, Cindy went on for ten minutes about how I almost died from falling out of the plane and how she would have died as well because she would not have known how to land.

The point is that risk to one person is business as usual to another. Investing one's savings in a new business almost always seems daring to a person who has never started a business. Better to leave that money in a savings account where it is safe. To someone with entrepreneurial experience, leaving it in savings so that inflation can reduce its purchasing power is much riskier.

One of the best books I have ever read on the subject of fear is *Feel the Fear and Do It Anyway*, by Susan Jeffers (1987). Jeffers states the case bluntly. "We cannot escape fear. We can only transform it into a companion that accompanies us on all our exciting adventures." We sometimes think that if we only had courage, we would not feel so scared. Honest people who have accomplished great things will tell you that fear never leaves us completely.

Coming to terms with fear allows us to consider options we may never have considered. Had I allowed fear to rule, I would have stayed on the farm. As it turns out, I would have had to leave anyway—the farm had to be sold a year or so later. Had I stayed, I would have faced much worse circumstances than I did by leaving on my own. Had I let my first failure dictate my future attempts, I would never have discovered that I could make money with my own business. Worse, I would always have harbored the feeling that I was not good enough or smart enough to make it as an entrepreneur.

The odd thing about courage is that no one can tell another person how to be courageous. Each of us must learn our own specific tolerance for risk and the circumstances under which fear is an accurate warning that our system gives us to avoid a catastrophe. However, our fear profile is malleable. We generally fear the unknown much more than the known. There is an old saying that goes, "The certainty of misery is better than the misery of uncertainty." Some therapists even say that fear of the unknown is the greatest fear of all.

When facing the prospect of starting a new business, there are countless skills and bits of knowledge that the inexperienced person may find overwhelming. When we perceive that we do not understand something, the tendency is to freeze. We act as if our ignorance were a permanent condition. It is not. As we learn about business, it becomes less of a mystery. Words that seemed unintelligible start to make sense. Ideas that were foreign to us become familiar. And, as we gain actual experience, we find that we are just as capable as the people we once thought had a direct line to some mystical business hotline.

The last positive virtue is independence of thought. Independence of thought does not mean never listening to others. Learning from others is invaluable. Relying on others to make our decisions is deadly. The next time you feel intimidated by someone with more financial knowledge, just remember all the whiz kids who bankrupted our major financial institutions. Any reasonably intelligent person with a desire to learn can master all that is necessary to run a small business.

Being independent means not going along with the crowd when you know better. Of course, all of us *say* we are independent. That is kind of like asking someone if they are a kind person. Even the biggest jackass in the county will *say* he is kind. When it comes down to acting on our best judgment rather than the popular sentiments we are soaked with every day, many of us at one time or another fold. We think in the back of our minds, "Well, maybe I don't know what I am talking about. Who am I to go against the judgment of everyone else?" How many times have you gone against your judgment when in the minority only to discover later that you were right all along?

Of course, sometimes we *are* wrong. Welcome to life. If we simply made an error, it's no big deal. If we were too mule-headed to listen to good advice, we probably should feel a little sheepish. If our doctor advises us to lose weight, cut back on the alcohol, and stop smoking and we keep eating like Henry VIII, drinking like a fish, and smoking like a chimney, we are just being dumb. If we examine the evidence, decide that we should spend half our advertising budget on radio and get no response, well, that is just a mistake.

Persistence, courage, and independence of thought all work together. As you develop one of these virtues it becomes easier to develop the others. A habit is hard to form but easy to maintain. As you make each of these a part of your deepest self, it becomes inconceivable that you would act in old, unproductive ways. The glue that binds these three virtues together is *integrity.* Thinking and acting congruently not only lets you sleep well at night—it allows others to plan their success around you, thus expanding your opportunities to prosper.

6 Playing Nice with Others

"Waste no more time arguing what a good man should be. Be one."
—*Marcus Aurelius*

 Recognizing that virtue involves other people is critical, but the core of virtue is your relationship with yourself. Polonius tells his son in Shakespeare's *Hamlet*, if you are true to yourself, you cannot be false to any man (Shakespeare, 2003). No one is an island, though. We operate in conjunction with others.

Robert Kiyosaki, author of *Rich Dad, Poor Dad*, is fond of saying that business is a team sport (Kiyosaki, 1997). He is right. No one person can hope to know or do everything when it comes to running a business. Even an author has a support staff of some kind. The editor, publishing agent, and other key people all contribute to an author's success.

Virtue in dealing with others involves predictability. If you say something, mean it. If you promise something, deliver it. If you cannot deliver on a promise, tell the affected person as soon as possible in the plainest way you can why you cannot deliver and when, if ever, you expect to be able to deliver.

The stock you build up with a reputation for dependability and honesty is worth more than any other stock you will ever hold. When you need a chance and do not have the resources to follow through, other people can be a great benefit if they know they can trust you to deliver.

Most people know that lying outright is wrong. I don't think this is the area most of us need work on. Most of us need work on the little things that do not seem like lies at the time we tell them. For example, say

I promise to deliver an order to a customer within a week. My supplier drops the ball, and it turns out that it will take three weeks to get the item. I know that my customer will cancel the order and get it elsewhere if he knows that it will be three weeks. So, instead of 'fessing up completely, I tell him the order has been delayed "for a few days." Is that a lie? Well, not exactly. Three weeks is a few days, kind of.

Now what happens when it turns out to be three weeks? I have one hopping mad customer, for one thing. For another, I have now sullied my reputation. Was the delay my fault? No. Should I have to pay for my supplier's mistake? Why does that matter? If all you think about is how to escape blame, you should not be in business.

So what *is* the right thing to do? If you know the whole score, share it with your customer. A three-week delay is a three-week delay. You may lose one order, but if your customer knows you can be trusted to tell the truth, you will stand a much better chance of getting the next one. If you fudge the truth, you may retain this order and lose all your potential ones in the future.

Developing the virtues of persistence, courage, and independence of thought along with developing your integrity in dealing with others is critical to your success, but they do not compare to the core virtue— honesty with yourself. We human beings are odd creatures. In the words of Nathaniel Branden, we are the only animal that can know what is good for itself and do precisely the opposite (Branden, 1997). Let's look at some of the ways we lie to ourselves.

Get rich quick

There is an old joke about the guy who bought a best-selling book entitled *Get Rich Quick*. Within the book was plenty of information, but none on getting rich. Puzzled, he tracked down the author to ask how to become rich quick. The author answered, "Write a book entitled *Get Rich Quick*."

Recent research indicates that few great things happen all at once. Geoff Colvin's (2008) research on world-class performers from a wide variety of fields shows that they generally have at least ten years of solid experience behind them. Bill Gates spent tens of thousands of hours programming computers before he started Microsoft. The Beatles were playing London pubs for years before making it big in Britain and the U.S. Behind every "overnight" success, you can bet there are years of preparatory work.

Even more noteworthy is the fact that among people who—against all probability—do achieve sudden success, few have *lasting* success. For example, people who win the lottery overwhelmingly find themselves after a few years right back where they started or even worse off. Winners of talent contests like American Idol often drift back into the legions of the barely known (Colvin, 2008).

There are a multitude of reasons to start your own business. Each person must find his/her own rock-bottom reason, and it usually is not what you first think it is. When I was in commission-only sales, I made a monthly list of goals. Usually my biggest items were a new car, gadgets, and other toys. Nothing wrong with that, mind you, but in retrospect, I was being untrue to myself. I had those things on my list because I thought I *should* have them on there. My mentor at the time was a very materialistic person. The only example I had other than the ultra-conservatism of the farm was him. So I modeled my goals after his. They did not work very well.

Later in life, after I had been a professor for some years, I read *Rich Dad, Poor Dad*. This turned out to be one of the most important books I ever read. In it, Robert Kiyosaki explained the Rat Race and how most of us live from paycheck to paycheck instead of building lasting wealth. He described a way of thinking about money that had never occurred to me. Money can be measured in time. That is, we can think of a particular amount of money as the amount of time it would last us if our income went to zero.

Then it hit me. I did not want showy wealth. Oh, sure, I like nice things. But all in all, my pickup gets me where I want to go, and my three bedroom, two bath house is perfectly adequate. I have no need to prove anything to anyone. Frankly, I never did—I just thought I did. So why accumulate wealth?

I learned (actually, *relearned*) that you can never achieve someone else's goal. Following Kiyosaki's advice, I set my goal to become financially independent. What does that mean? Well, in *Rich Dad* language, that means having enough money coming in from passive income to cover all my living expenses. I am not there yet, but I will be. I know that because I have something important and meaningful *to me*—my family. Best of all, I am doing it without sacrificing time with my family, my health, or my spiritual growth.

I have learned the power of patience. When I was young and broke, I hated the feeling of helplessness and failure. I wanted it to change, and I wanted it to change instantly. Though I achieved many of my goals, financial ones included, I never made the progress I was capable of. It took me years to understand why. I was busy trying to escape legitimate suffering. Instead of building the foundation of character and knowledge that would allow me to support my financial growth, I wanted to stop the pain. When you only focus on relieving yourself of pain, you forgo the chance to learn. You are also tempted to take shortcuts, ethical and otherwise. In the end, this approach almost never works.

If your motivation for starting a new business is that you are broke, be careful. If you think that this is the easiest way to stop the calls from creditors or dig yourself out of massive debt, slow down and think it through. The road to financial freedom is littered with those who got in a hurry and failed to build a foundation of good character and knowledge.

Seeing what you want to see

We lie to ourselves—all the time. Some people look in the mirror and see a slim, svelte stud muffin when the rest of the world sees a pudgy couch potato. Others look and see an overweight slob even when they are already too skinny. Few of us are completely objective when it comes to our habits and ourselves. The world is what it is, but we interpret it according to our preconceived notions of what we hope or fear it to be.

One of the most enduring ethics guides in history is the *Dhammapada*, teachings of the Buddha. I enjoy reviewing the Eightfold Path because it is so simple and so common sense. One of its central messages is that suffering is reduced when we stop trying to interpret the world in terms of what we wish or fear. When we see things simply and directly, without unnecessary complications, we are able to deal with it matter-of-factly. When we force our notions of what "should" be onto situations, we inevitably make things harder for ourselves.

I see these tendencies regularly when I work with entrepreneurs. One of the biggest problems is getting them to understand that what customers *should* want is often different from what they *do* want. An entrepreneur often become so enamored of his or her product that they forget they have to have customers to make a successful business.

Another tendency is to ignore bad news in the name of "positive thinking." Let me admit first that I have been a student of positive thinking for many, many years. Understood correctly, it is one of the most powerful life-improvement tools available. Adjusting one's attitude is, in fact, a precursor to any lasting success. However, there is a dark side to the whole Positive Mental Attitude movement. Often it becomes like a cult in which all "negative" thoughts are banned from discussion. Anyone who dares to bring up ugly facts is labeled a negative person. I ran around with my share of these folks when I was young and foolish. Guess what? Most of them fell by the wayside because time after time they ignored bad news instead of facing it courageously.

What is the alternative? Simple dealing with reality. News is news. Facts are facts. If you insist on reality conforming to your expectations, you are likely to become an anxious, fault-finding person.

The gambler's fallacy

The root cause of our fooling ourselves is pattern-seeking. Similar to seeing what we want to see, we often fall victim to imposing patterns on events or series of events that really *have* no pattern. I use a neat demonstration in my classes to demonstrate this irresistible tendency. First, I play a section of a Led Zeppelin song backwards (these can be found on any number of web sites) and ask if anyone heard any words. Inevitably, they hear the word "Satan." This sound is completely random, mind you, but sure enough, it *sounds* like the word "Satan." Then I show the "words" to the song played backwards. Someone with more time than sense has figured out some satanic-sounding lines to go with the random sounds they hear. Now here's the kicker. Once you "hear" those words, you can never again *not* hear the words. If you don't believe me, try it.

How does this apply to your business? Well, have you ever had a streak of bad luck and said to yourself that it's about time for your luck to change? Here's some startling news (I hope you are sitting down). There is no pattern. Aside from the fact that the concept of luck is questionable anyway, previous good fortune generally has nothing to do with future good fortune. Casino owners know this. They know something else, too. In addition to our tendency to throw good money after bad, we tend to do the opposite when things are going well. After a streak of success, we often think it will continue.

In business, this can be disastrous. I learned this lesson the hard way when I lost all my money in my first venture. In reality, all indications were that the business could not succeed about ninety days before it actually folded. Yet I continued to pour every last dime into it, thinking I could turn it around. Remember the section on persistence versus stupidity? Well, this was the latter.

What happens during a run of *good* fortune? Many times we get lazy. We start messing up on the fundamentals. We think we know it all. And then, we get clobbered. Even big companies fall prey to this tendency. I admired Microsoft for years, and I used their products almost exclusively. Eventually, though, they started to take things for granted. They released software that was not a hit with consumers because it had problems and was not anything really new. Their ads started to convey a feeling of desperation. Though they will no doubt be around for a long time, it is clear that they have become soft.

Paralysis by analysis

Too much of a good thing is a bad thing. While I advocate doing a good analysis of a business before investing a lot of time and money into it, I also recognize that there is a point at which action beats reflection. I hesitate to say this because many people go off half-cocked and unnecessarily lose their money.

The best example I have of someone who thinks too much was an entrepreneur I advised some years ago. He had a stunning product. It was unique and hard to duplicate. We identified ways to market it. He refined the product, and then he refined it some more. When he was through refining it, he would investigate trade shows. Then he would investigate some more trade shows. In the end, he just did not have the fire in the belly that it takes to be a success. He took a job as a kindergarten teacher and never pursued the idea again.

I see dozens of ideas every year. Very few of them are worth a dime. This one was, and yet the founder was unable to get past analysis; don't let this happen to you.

Imagine yourself on a road in the woods and you can only see to the next bend in the road. You don't stop and examine all the possibilities that may lie before you. You walk on until you can see what is around the bend. It may be inviting or it may be scary. It may be rough or it may be smooth. The point is you can't *know* until you step around that corner. In business, we can only get so many answers before we get out there and screw up. Only by screwing up can you hope to make necessary adjustments to your business model.

Awareness, acceptance and action

Three steps are necessary to inoculate yourself against faulty thinking. I call it the 3A method. The first step is AWARENESS. Awareness is the easiest of the three, at least in principle. All you have to do is pay attention. Now if you think this is easy in practice, you probably have not actually tried it. You see, our mental lives take place on different levels. Our conscious minds are extremely limited in their capacity. For example, have you ever wondered why phone numbers have seven digits (minus the area code)? It is because most of us can only retain about seven items in working memory (Baddeley, 2004). So where is all that other stuff we supposedly know?

Well, it is there, but we are not aware of it unless we need it. In fact, much of what we know can direct our actions without our being aware of it at all. Think about learning to ride a bicycle. At first, you had to be aware of pedaling, switching the handlebars back and forth to keep your balance, and looking ahead for obstacles. Kept you pretty busy, huh? But then, after a few practices, you were going down the street like a pro, showing off to your friends. At that point, you do not need to think about what you are doing—you just do it. The part you do not have to think about is stored in your subconscious mind.

Along with skills like bike riding, other things reside in our sub-conscious minds. We do not see each situation in life as completely new. We have learned certain patterns of behavior that guide us to react in basically the same way in similar situations. Thank heaven for that. If it were not so, we could never do anything very complicated. That seven-item limit would limit us to only the simplest of tasks. Now, if you were lucky enough to have learned only good stuff during your lifetime, you are fine. Don't change a thing. Also, I feel for you. It must be lonely being the only person on the planet like that.

The rest of us need help. We came away from childhood with literally thousands of behavior patterns. Some were good. Most of us learned pretty early not to touch a hot stove; that kept us safe. We also learned some basic assumptions about life, and this is where we ran into trouble. Sometimes the people we were around the most had bad attitudes. They may have been good people who held some bad assumptions.

One example is people who think their income is limited. This has been a big one for me. I grew up in a lower middle class environment.

We always had plenty of what we needed, but never enjoyed many luxuries. Though when I left the farm because I wanted to increase my income, it took me years to overcome my subconscious limitations. I still fight that, frankly. With each new level of income, I find myself having to make adjustments in my subconscious assumptions.

The problem is that we are often not aware of these patterns. We rarely stop to think about what may be driving our daily behavior. This is where awareness comes in. Here's an exercise. Next time you make a significant decision, stop for a moment. I don't mean a decision like what to do with the rest of your life, but just some routine decision that is more important than which shoes to wear. Notice that just underneath your conscious mind some thoughts are rushing by, barely noticeable. Without straining, just notice them a little more. Within a few seconds, one or two of these thoughts will emerge into your conscious mind. Do not judge the thoughts, determining that this one is "good" or that one is "bad." Just notice that they are there.

Now ask yourself, "How is this barely-noticed thought influencing my decision?" Let's go back to my case. When I have the opportunity to make more money, I have two things going on in my mind simultaneously. The most noticeable is the resounding "yes" that tells me I really like the idea. The less noticeable is the doubt and borderline guilt. For me, that subtle thought is a vague feeling that somehow I do not belong among the ranks of the wealthy.

Origins of thoughts like these are sometimes hard to figure out, but in this case, I have come to the conclusion that it was just by example. I never was told that wealthy people were bad; I was just never around any. I had no idea what it was like to have a lot of money and to be surrounded by nice things. Add to that the fact that if I were to exceed what my father had done, I would in a sense be belittling him. I know, I know. This doesn't make sense, and my father would never have thought that for a minute. Nonetheless, subconscious thoughts have to be evaluated as they are, not as we think they should be.

The good news is that these thoughts can be redirected. I often relax and just imagine how it would be to have the level of wealth I really want. It does not matter whether I believe it at the time. I just have to let my subconscious mind get used to a new reality. Slowly but surely, my undercurrent of thoughts has shifted to a stream of images and ideas that support wealth rather than fight against it. Most importantly, it is the kind of wealth that is right for *me*. Remember, you can't reach someone else's goals.

How does this translate into business? I see countless business owners who really don't have a clue how well (or how poorly) they are doing. One reason is just plain laziness—people don't tend to keep good records because recordkeeping takes work and is hardly ever as exciting as doing something else. But there is another reason, one I discovered a few years ago. I noticed that I was pretty good about keeping my checkbook balanced some months, but in others I was abysmal. I got to noticing that it was easy to stay caught up when I had plenty of money, but hard when I had a tight month. When is it more important to know where you stand? Well, it is important all the time, but it is critical when money is tight. We all, on some level, want to avoid bad news.

ACCEPTANCE is the second of the 3A fundamentals. This one is more subtle, though we were introduced to it a paragraph or two ago. First, we must understand what acceptance is *not*—it is not *liking* a situation. You may accept that you could lose a few pounds even though you dislike it. Nor is it *approving* of a situation. I disapprove of politicians and terrorists, but I accept that they exist and that they have at least some effect on my life. Accepting is simply not fighting reality. If you have been reading too much post-modern thought, you may be confused on what reality is. My favorite quote on this subject is attributed to Philip Dick, "Reality is whatever refuses to go away when I stop believing in it."

Look around you at the people you know and meet every day. For the moment, leave yourself out of it. Don't worry—we'll get to you shortly. Notice how many of them seem to be indignant. Some are obvious about it; some are subtle. Indignation creeps up wherever there is a "should" hanging around. "People shouldn't park so close to my car." Well, maybe they shouldn't, but they do. "My students should be more motivated." Well, they aren't. "The government shouldn't spend so much money." Don't get me going on that one... oops. See, we *all* have the tendency to "should" all over everybody.

So what's wrong with that? Look at it this way. You have only so much mental, emotional, physical and spiritual energy. Do you want to spend it on things you cannot possibly control, or would you rather spend it on things you *can* change? It's your choice.

One of my favorite proverbs is from Nigeria. "Truth is a bitter herb. Many cannot eat." Once we accept that something is true, we remove a drain on our limited mental and spiritual resources. The Serenity Prayer is hard to improve upon:

Grant me the serenity to accept the things I cannot change
The courage to change the things I can
And the wisdom to know the difference.

Acceptance also loosens us up. We start letting life come at us without tensing up and expecting to get knocked backwards. When I was a teenager, my cousins and I agreed to help one of our neighbors, J.W., put up his hay. For those of you who missed out on this experience, let me describe it. Imagine a July day at about ninety-five degrees and a relative humidity of about the same. Think of moving forty- to sixty-pound bales of hay from the ground to a wagon and then from the wagon to the loft of a barn. A loft is like the second story in a barn. Did I say ninety-five degrees? That was the outside temperature. Inside that loft it was more like 115. My cousins and I chipped in cheerfully (more or less) and helped J.W. get his hay in. About the time we were finished, J.W. sits on a bale, sweat running down his face, and says, "You know, doing this wasn't half as bad as dreading it."

As you might guess, I was in no mood for philosophy. Aside from the heat and the physical exhaustion, breathing hay dust had my allergies in high gear, and I was wondering why we were being so stinking generous. Doubled over at the knees from sneezing and fatigue, I felt like making some smart remark but did not have the energy to follow through. As we got in the truck and headed home, the message sank in. J.W. was not being particularly philosophical. He was just noticing something about himself. And what he noticed started to ring true for me. I began to see that I, too, had a tendency to dread distasteful tasks, but that they were almost never as bad as I imagined them. With a little practice we start to realize, like J.W., that dreading something is much worse than experiencing it.

Last, acceptance puts the present moment in a different light. No matter how bad things are, if we can accept that they *are* the way they are, we can get down to business and start working on the future. We may not be able to control the future completely, but we have more influence on it than we do the past. Whether our present situation is the result of things we could have done better, or events that were more or less imposed on us, acceptance paves the way for *action*, the third part of the 3A program.

ACTION is the thing that makes awareness and acceptance worth the price. Sure, we could become spiritually stronger if we were to simply become more aware and accepting. In fact, I would even say that if we were *just* to do those two things our lives would become immeasurably better. The reason is that by enlarging our consciousness, we make it harder to do things that are clearly against our self-interest. If we refuse to deny that we exercise too little by blocking it from our awareness, it becomes harder to continue the lie. If we accept that fact non-judgmentally, we may find ourselves exercising regularly without really trying.

For the most part, though, action requires a conscious effort. When it comes time to act, there is no substitute for simply deciding to get specific things done. Time management is a large topic, and I recommend you study it constantly. However, there is one tip that exceeds all the others.

It comes from David Allen's *Getting Things Done* (Allen, 2003). Time management is feeling good about what you are *not* doing.

When I first read that idea, I stopped short. Most of the dozens upon dozens of books I had read over the years had basically the same message—make a list of things to do and do the most important ones first. Allen's book has many of the same types of recommendations. But this idea was new to me. As I reflected on the passage, I laughed at how many times I had been doing one thing while subconsciously wondering if I ought to be doing something else.

It took me a long time to integrate this deceptively simple rule into my life. I have a wide range of interests, and it is sometimes difficult for me to accept the fact that I can never learn everything I want to know and do everything I want to do. Little by little, though, I have come to realize that focusing on a few important projects at a time and letting the others go for the present makes life infinitely more enjoyable and considerably less stressful.

As you start your new business, remember that every single day there will be more things to do (more correctly things you *think* you have to do) than you can possibly get done. Become *aware* of that fact, *accept* that it is that way, and *act* on those things that in your judgment top all the others in importance. Then go to bed at night knowing you did the best you could.

 # Surviving the Early Going

"There are basically two types of people. People who accomplish things, and people who claim to have accomplished things. The first group is less crowded."

—*Mark Twain*

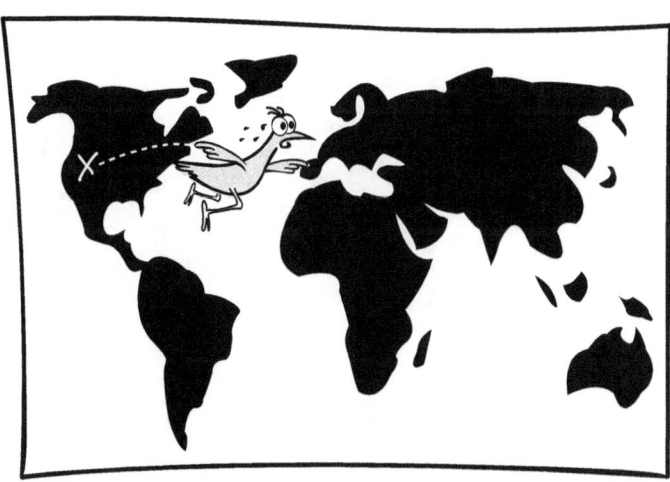

 So now you have your business open. What are the things you need to think about during your first year in business? First and foremost, remember this phrase: Cash is King. Repeat after me. Cash is King. Cash is King. Many great ideas have gone by the wayside because they were not sufficiently funded or because it took longer than expected to reach positive cash flow. Had cash been managed properly, they probably would have been hugely successful.

In addition to cash, a business must have a viable structure and a set of business systems to survive. Doing things willy-nilly may be OK for a hobby but not for a business. It is the daily discipline of doing the right things the right way that makes a business the best it can be. It is no guarantee of success, but failing to set up the right systems is a guarantee of failure.

Calculating your start up cash

Let's face it. If you had enough cash, you wouldn't be starting this business, right? I sometimes kid my students by suggesting they save $250,000 or so before they graduate so they have start up money ready to go. Or, as the old joke goes, if I had some money, I could buy gas to put in my car—if I had a car. Yet we all know that it is next-to-impossible to start a business without at least some cash. Take the following story.

An ad appeared in the local paper of a mid-sized city. It was nondescript—just a regular ad in the classified section. All it said was, "Last day to send in your dollar." That's it. No promise of

anything, just an invitation to send cash. The person who placed the
ad received thousands of one-dollar bills in the mail. You can't get
much more cost-effective than that. But even that business had a
start up cost, namely writing and placing the ad. Before you get any
bright ideas, the perpetrator also got an invitation to jail. Now, in
my view, there was no fraud because nothing was promised. Further,
anyone who would send in a dollar on the basis of such an ad should
be separated from it. My opinion won't keep you out of jail, though.

Even if your cash outlay is literally zero, which can happen for a
service business, your time is worth something. If you weren't doing
this business, you could be doing something else to earn money. In
economic terms, that is called an opportunity cost. Tutoring kids is an
example. All you need is your brain and some time.

For most businesses, we have to buy some things to get started. If
we don't buy them, we have to borrow them. And if we borrow them,
we are banking on being able to pay that back from the revenues
generated by the business. There is nothing wrong with that, but we
have to remember that we are not changing the fact that there are
start up costs. We are just adjusting the point in time at which we
have to actually pay them.

How much money do you need? That depends on what you are trying
to accomplish. If you just want to test out a concept, spend only what
you need to make a few things and sell them. I once worked with a
start-up that sold specialty beef. It was from organically-raised cattle.
The founder got a slaughtered cow from a relative with the promise
to pay when he had made enough sales. He got the proper licenses

and cooked up some steaks and burgers for samples to give away at a college football game. He also provided order forms for cuts of meat. Given the response, it appeared there was a market, signaling that it was time for the next step. Mission accomplished.

Often, the concept is already tested or the business model is well known. Let's say someone wants to open a clothing store. We know they work, or at least some of them do. How do we figure the amount that they will need to get this business going? We do it in three steps.

First, we add up the costs of everything we need to open. Anything we spend money for before we open the doors for business goes in the *start-up cost* category. Here is a list of some typical start up expenses:

$ 2,500	Lease deposit
+ $ 100,000	Inventory
+ $ 2,500	Insurance
+ $ 10,000	Wages during training
+ $ 5,000	Pre-opening advertising
$120,000	**Total start-up expenses**

Of course, this list may not be complete, but it allows us to see how quickly expenses add up before we even open the doors for business. So we know we need at least $120,000 before we make our first dollar of revenue.

Next, we add up our projected revenues, based on some reasonable assumptions about our future performance. Remember that in

Chapter 4, we discussed how to make reasonable projections of both revenues and expenses. We also learned how to calculate cash flow and cash balance. With this information, we can figure out how much money the business needs to get it through its first few months of existence. We do this by looking for our lowest cash balance based on our projections.

Let's say that we open January 1 and for the first six months, we spend more money than we bring in. This is not unusual, by the way, though most small business owners do not plan for negative cash flow. Obviously, that means that if we only invest that $120,000 in our business (the total of our start up expenses) we will be bouncing checks the first month! Not good. So we look across our pro forma cash flow statement (remember that *pro forma* is a *pro*-jection) and find the month in which we have the lowest cash balance. In this case, that number will be negative. The amount of money it takes to get that "lowest cash balance" up to zero is then added to our start up expenses. Think of it as the amount of money necessary to fund a negative cash flow.

But wait, what if we are off by a little? Murphy's Law prevails. You can bet things will go wrong. We need to build in a cash cushion. That amount is determined by adding up all the expenses that will have to be paid month by month even if we have no revenues coming in. How could that happen? Think 9/11 or Hurricane Katrina. How many months? Good question. Ideally, six months cash reserves should be available. But is that realistic? Probably not. I use three months as a rule of thumb. If everything were to come crashing down, I know the business could remain open for three months. When my cash reserves get lower than that, I start acting to bring them back up right away.

Managing cash

In the early stages of your business, treat every dollar as if it were your last. Psychologically, this is harder than it sounds, especially if you have worked hard to get an investor. You go from a bank account balance of near-zero to having several thousand dollars instantly and the penny-pinching attitude you had at first melts overnight. It is easy to think about how much nicer your office would be with an expensive print on the wall or a mahogany file cabinet. Resist that urge.

On the other hand, you can be too cheap on the things that really do matter. A few extra dollars spent on paint and attractive signage can make the difference between looking like a professional or a rank amateur. Nothing gives a bad first impression quite like one of those rolling trailer-type signs with letters missing parked at the side of the road. The message is something like, "We don't care enough to be professional; please buy from us anyway." Just as coffee stains on your airplane tray make you wonder if they maintain the engines poorly, an unattractive facade can make you wonder if the owner sells trash. Is that fair? It doesn't matter! You are judged by how you first look to a prospective customer and that first impression often outweighs all the rest.

And for heaven's sake, keep the place clean! We get used to the clutter and filth in a place we inhabit constantly. To everyone else, we look like pigs. I learned this lesson shortly after I left the farm and had my own business. My upbringing was fairly traditional, and so men did not generally clean around the house. I knew in theory that toilets got cleaned, but in practice this was a foreign idea. My mentor at the time walked out from the bathroom in my new martial arts school and pointed out that students and visitors might not find toilet stains very attractive. From then on, I realized just how blind we are to our own dirt and how noticeable it is to others.

Another pitfall of the early stages of a business is shortsightedness. If you use a line of credit, for example, it is easy to treat this money the same as cash. Wrong. Every debt dollar you use becomes a millstone around your neck. This does not mean debt is bad. Debt is a tool, and like most tools it can be misused. When cash is flowing in like mad, it is easy to trick yourself into believing it will last forever. Then the off-season hits and you watch helplessly as you cash balance nears zero. If you have already used up your credit line, you are hosed.

Your most important use of cash during the first two or three years of business is growth. I do not mean rapid, uncontrolled growth or growing beyond your capabilities of managing. I mean that every dollar should be spent with the idea of making your business a winning enterprise, one that has a consistent positive cash flow. Then, and only then, should you spend for anything unnecessary. What is necessary and what is not is a judgment call. Should you buy a delivery van for your flower business? That depends. If the primary contact customers have with you is the van (say you are a delivery-only business), it may pay to have a nice one with your logo on the doors. If you sell out of a storefront and deliver only occasionally, your personal vehicle might serve you better.

Tracking your finances

Another area where I recommend you *not* scrimp is financial advice. The first step is to make sure you are tracking your cash and following the law. For the most part, these two things can be handled by a bookkeeper. Why spend money on a bookkeeper when you can do it yourself? For the same reason that you should not act as your own lawyer—you don't want an idiot as a client.

This is especially true in the case of taxes. One year, I decided that paying someone to do my taxes was unnecessary. I carefully filled out my forms, which were quite simple, or so I thought. I reported everything, but I reported some outside income on the wrong line. Three years later, Uncle Sam asked me for $3,000. Ouch. Never again did I try to do my own taxes, even when they were dead simple.

At what point do you need a bookkeeper? I recommend as early as is feasible. If you are just testing a market and not really working your business yet, it may be OK to track your own finances as long as you get good tax advice. Once any appreciable amount of money starts changing hands, it's time for help.

Bookkeepers generally do the menial tasks of consolidating information from your checkbook register into an income statement and balance sheet. Insist that they do a cash flow statement as well. Beyond that, they are generally not trained to give financial advice. For that, you need a financial advisor. Certified Public Accountants are trained not only to consolidate your information but also to render specific advice on money management.

A note of caution here—if you go to the phone book and look up financial advisors, the vast majority of listings will be for people selling investment instruments. Their primary objective is to sell you something. There is nothing wrong with that, but you should know how they make their money before hiring them.

Other kinds of financial advisors work on a fee basis. They are not trying to sell you anything because they do not have anything to sell except their services. Again, caution is in order, because some of these advisors specialize in personal rather than business finances. The best bet is someone who has experience in small business advising and who can give you a good list of references.

No matter how good your advisors are, they are never a substitute for your own judgment. I have met any number of small business owners who turn over their bookkeeping to someone else, trusting that they will make the right decisions about money. They want to forget about the numbers so they can get on with doing business. Part of me is sympathetic. After all, if you wanted to be an accountant, you would have become one. But this is a colossally bad idea. You and only you can manage your business. Letting other people do it for you is bound to lead to a disaster because they won't suffer if it fails. All they lose is one customer. You may lose everything.

We will discuss business systems in general shortly, but financial systems are especially important. With today's point-of-sale systems, bookkeeping programs, and training material, there is absolutely no excuse for not having a minute-to-minute or at least a day-to-day read on your cash position. Watch it like a hawk.

Spending priorities

The first priority of a business is the same as that of a human being in general—survival. When it is impossible to pay all your bills, something almost all businesses experience at one time or another, you have to decide which ones to pay. If you are like me, you take your promises seriously. When I take out a loan, I consider that a promise I gave freely, and I do everything I can to keep it. When I get supplies on credit, I do my level best to pay on time, as promised.

On the other hand, there are expenses that are important, but not contractual. Advertising comes to mind. When cash gets tight, we look down our list of bills payable and see that big expense staring us in the face. Our first instinct is to cut back on advertising and promotional expenses in order to leave enough money to pay the bank and suppliers. While this *sounds* like the right thing to do, it often is exactly the wrong thing to do. Cutting back on advertising will usually exacerbate a cash problem, especially if it is the result of lower revenues. Consider carefully whether it is better to make the bank wait while you get revenues back up or to make a bad situation worse by scrimping on ads.

Another category that seems optional is employee compensation. Years ago, I worked as a sales manager for a company that was run by accountants. I am not knocking accountants as a whole, but in general I have observed that they see the world through a lens of cost-cutting. I proposed a program whereby I would help my salespeople close sales and get an override on the commissions. In other words, I would be getting paid to help others close sales. I benefited only when the company (and my salespeople) benefited.

The first month, my club (this was a health club) broke every sales record ever set for that location. I had proven my point, or so I thought. The next month, they canceled the program and put me back to earning only my own commission with a small manager's salary. Why? It turns out the accountants up top saw my salary for that month and freaked out. All they could see was the expense. What they could not see was that revenues were higher than ever! Don't ask me to explain that one. I have thought it over for years, and stupidity is still the best explanation I can come up with.

Training is another expense category that gets cut too soon. When times are tough, many businesses resort to the "warm bodies" principle. If they can breathe and have a pulse, they can work here. We'll train them when we get ahead on cash. Wrong thing to do. As your employees' competence goes down, so do your revenues. This one may take longer to show up, but it is deadly. And, unlike advertising and compensation, it takes a long time to correct.

Payroll

When we think of a successful business, we often picture scores of employees all working together for a common purpose. Some people even measure business size in terms of number of employees. While this *can* be an indication of success, it can also mean you have a bloated staff. What is important is not how many people you have, but how much cash flow they contribute.

There are two categories of employees—line and staff. Line people contribute directly to the production of whatever the business makes. A wagon wheel manufacturer may have a "line" of managers and employees underneath him or her. Each is directly responsible for making wheels or directly supervising those who do. The people shipping the wheels support production in a sense, but they don't actually make wheels. They are called "staff."

Chances are, you don't need staff for some time. In fact, you may not need as many line people as you think. I know of one multi-million business that employees only five people. Not bad, huh?

How do you know when to hire and when not to hire? A lot depends on your business model. Say you sell flowers. There is any number of ways to sell flowers. Let's look at three different versions of that basic idea. Each represents a different business model.

First, you could open a flower shop. This model involves customers coming in physically to a store, looking at flowers, choosing which to buy, and paying you at the counter. Nothing mysterious or complicated here—this is just a regular old flower shop. How many employees do you need?

Obviously, someone has to be present at all times the shop is open. That someone may be you at first. Up to a certain sales volume, a single person may be able to handle everything. For example, if you buy your flowers wholesale, arrange them in the store, and then sell them, you may only need to staff the store yourself. Time between serving customers can be used to make arrangements. If you need a break, pick one hour (usually not lunch time, when customers find it convenient to shop) to close.

If sales grow, and you are going to make sure they do, there will come a point at which you need to have help. Some small business owners try to start with a large staff and everything they need to be a big store right away. The problem is, cash flow at first rarely supports their overhead. This translates into a negative cash flow for an extended period of time. A negative cash flow has to be funded from the business's initial investment, which means you have to have more to get started. All in all, it is best to avoid this scenario. Start by doing everything you can yourself, work out the bugs, and hire only as you acquire the wisdom and the resources to grow.

A second business model might be a flower delivery service. In this model, customers go online or place their orders by phone and you deliver the flowers. This is a case in which it is hard to start solo. Delivering takes time, and someone has to take the orders while another person delivers. Nonetheless, two people could probably do this business for some time, at least until there are too many orders for one delivery person to handle.

But wait. There are alternatives. If there is a local courier service, you might employ them on a contract basis to deliver for you. Alternatively, you might deliver them yourself and have contract workers in their homes do the arrangements.

A third business model is to sell flowers wholesale. You grow them and sell to retailers. Again, the question is how many people are absolutely necessary to conduct business while you grow.

No matter what business model you settle on, there is one standard way to calculate whether to hire an additional person. The amount of revenue generated from the additional person must exceed the total of *all* costs associated with the new hire. In order to understand this concept, we need to expand our knowledge of finance.

8 Growing Wisely

> "You've got to do your own growing, no matter how tall your grandfather was."
>
> —*Irish Saying*

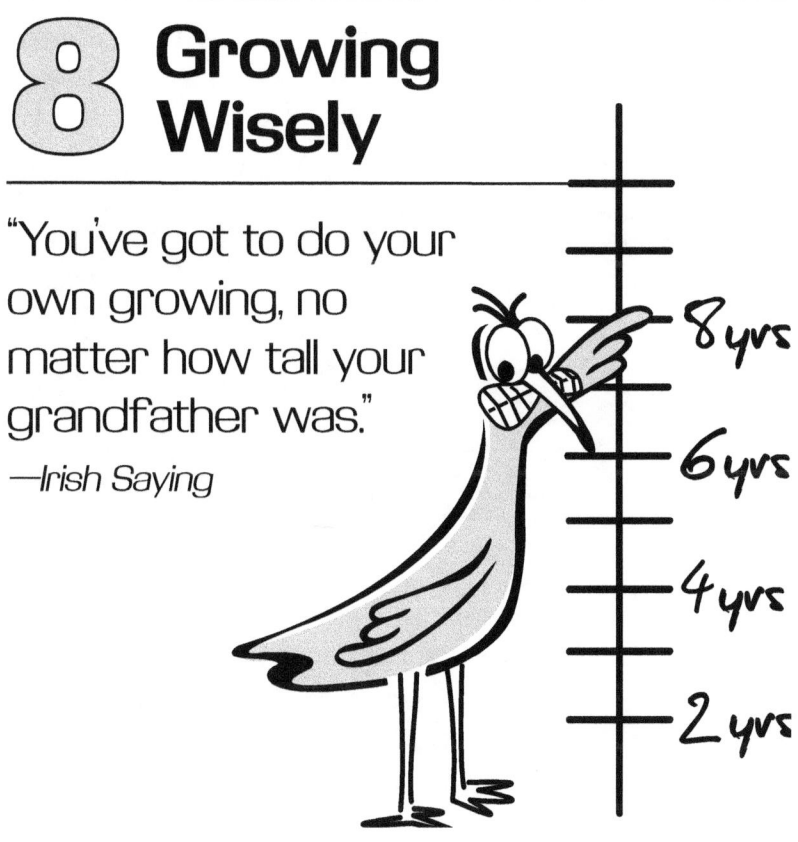

8 yrs

6 yrs

4 yrs

2 yrs

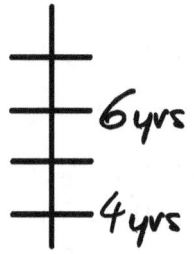

Now you're open. Whew! What a relief. All that planning and scraping up resources worked, and you are the proud owner of a new business. Congratulations!

Now you face a different set of demands. Growth can make or break a new business. We all tend to think that growth is good, and it is. Unbridled growth, though, is a disaster. There was a great commercial a few years ago during the dot.com craze. A new company launched its web site and anxiously watched hits on the web counter. At first, there was elation as hit after hit came in. Then the hits kept coming and kept coming and kept coming. As they passed the 100,000 mark, looks of joy turned to horror. How would they fill all the orders?

Each stage of growth brings with it a new set of accomplishments *and* problems. This is not far different from life in general. We all know from experience that growing up is painful. Remember those teen years when all the excitement of becoming independent and going out on your own was intermingled with the terror of facing problems on your own? Remember how with each new relationship you learned painfully how hard it is to be a good mate? *Expecting* growth to be filled with challenges goes a long way toward making it tolerable, if not exactly pleasant.

Why do so many small businesses stagnate? Take a walk down the main street of your town or city. Notice the stores and shops along the way. How many are barely making it? With a little practice, you can tell a lot about the finances of a store just by observing. What does the facade look like? Is it attractive and well kept? How about the employees? Do they look happy and helpful or do they look like extras from *Dawn of the Dead?*

Now, pick out three or four businesses to investigate further. Do your best to get a feel for their business processes—their systems. Watch someone purchase something or purchase something yourself. How are transactions handled? Do they still use a receipt pad? If so, are the receipts stacked neatly somewhere? Do they put them in a drawer? Are they mixed in with a pile of papers on the front desk? If they use a computerized point-of-sale system, notice how items are tallied for purchases. Do they scan them with a bar code? Do they look up an item number and enter it manually?

Next, look at the general tenor and tone of operations. Do people look like they know what they are doing? Do the floor personnel have to constantly ask someone else how to do something? Are they happy and helpful or clueless and grumpy? Does the store have the feel of a tightly run airplane cockpit or spring break in Ft. Lauderdale?

Many small business owners are not really growing a business. Instead, they have managed to create a horrible job for themselves. Most of their time is spent fighting fires and averting near-disasters. Many are in ill health from stress. *Worse, many of them have no idea that they are one bad month away from bankruptcy.*

Core employees

Since payroll is often one of the largest items on the expense side, let's look at it first. At the end of the last chapter, I admonished you only to hire someone if the increased revenues from the hire exceeded the full cost of the employee, all costs taken into account. Let's get more specific. We will examine core employees first, followed by what I call *support* employees. After that, we will look at the issue of growth in general.

Core employees are no mystery. They are the engine of the business, those without whom you cannot stay open. A hospital needs doctors. We also know that there are other kinds of workers who are essential to the functioning of a hospital, like receptionists, nurses, etc. But without doctors, nothing happens.

Your business also has essential hires, or core employees. For the moment, let's think of your business as a separate entity from you as a person. At this stage, we don't care whether you have actually created a separate entity legally. I just want you to think of it as separate and yourself as a hired employee or manager of that entity.

The first thing you need to realize is that you are not *necessarily* a core employee. Some entrepreneurs start businesses with no intention whatsoever of actually working in the business. In fact, your being a core employee often limits your ability to grow the business. More on that shortly.

Earlier, we talked about how to zero in on your business's value-added. Hopefully, you know what it is that you do best and how to delegate or outsource things you are not so good at to someone else. If not, revisit Chapter 2. Now, think about whom in your business actually does the value-added activity. Going back to the basket business example, the person or persons who make the baskets actually add the value. They are the doctors of this "hospital."

In an earlier chapter, we looked at margins. Margins, you will recall, are the amount of money we make on each unit of something we sell. If Betty pays ten dollars for the raw material for a basket, and then sells that basket for thirty dollars, her margin for each basket is twenty dollars. As we noted before, this is a very important figure when it comes to hiring. Let's see why.

Normally, we only include the actual cost of raw materials in our margin calculations. But we know that in reality, someone has to make those raw materials into a product that can be sold—baskets in this case. That person has to make enough baskets to justify his or her wage. If Tom can only make one basket an hour, the positive cash flow he generates is $20. In other words, twenty dollars is his value-added for one hour's work. Of course, we cannot pay him that much in reality because we have other costs to support our basket building—utilities, insurance, and so forth. The reason we want to know that number is that it defines the maximum we could theoretically pay Tom and still make money on his efforts.

At the risk of stating the obvious, it makes no sense to pay someone unless that person produces more in revenues than he or she costs the business. The easiest case to figure out is one like we just talked about. We can link Tom's efforts to a specific output. In fact, because Tom's hourly wage can easily be linked to his basket production, we could count Tom's wage as part of Cost of Goods Sold. Let's say we were to pay him $8 an hour and that he produced one basket an hour, day in and day out. Our margins would look like this:

```
  $ 30   Price of 1 basket
- $ 10   Cost of raw materials
- $  8   Tom's wage
─────────────────────────────
  $ 12   Gross margin
```

That means that for every hour we employ Tom, we make $12. Of course, we don't get to keep all that money, do we? No, we have to pay those other bills we talked about—the ones that we do not link directly to the production of one basket. So even though this is an incomplete picture of the effect of hiring Tom, it is an essential one. We have $12 an hour to "work with."

Support employees

Many businesses need non-core employees in order to run well. Going back to our example of the basket business, someone has to run the counter if the business is a retail store. However, calculating whether hiring a non-core employee is cost-effective is a little trickier than for a core employee. The first question to ask is whether we absolutely, positively have to have this employee to function. For example, could Tom make baskets *and* run the counter?

If we were running a business where sales only occurred once in a while, the answer would be easy. I once heard of a fellow who made a decent living selling life-size woodcarvings of Native Americans. He only made two or so a year, but they sold for a substantial sum. Obviously, he did not need someone to staff a counter all the time. He could easily help potential customers himself. On the other extreme, if our business were a candy store with low prices and high volume, the candy-maker could not come out of the kitchen to wait on customers constantly.

But what about hiring decisions that fall somewhere in between these two extremes? The trick is to figure out how much production is lost if a core employee takes care of non-core work. If Tom waits on customers, how many fewer baskets will he make on average? According to our figures above, he makes one basket an hour, which gives us $12 gross margin. If, say, half of his time is diverted to waiting on customers, we now only make $6 an hour gross margin.

The danger here is succumbing to the illusion that Tom's counter work is free. It actually costs us $6 an hour in lost revenue. Notice that this has nothing to do with Tom's actual wage. His wage for a half-hour is $4, but having him wait on customers half the time costs us $6.

What can we do with that information? Well, in practical terms it means that we can hire someone for $6 an hour to run the counter and still make $6 gross margin. Either way, we make the same amount of money. We might think at first that this is a perfectly even trade-off, but that is partially an illusion. It is an even trade-off as long as we stay at the same level of sales, but when we grow to the point where we need another production person, things change for the better.

Let's say we hire Mary. Mary can make the same number of baskets as Tom—one per hour. Therefore, if we add her to the payroll, we add $12 to our gross margin. When we hired Tom, we only made $6 gross margin in the end, because we had to have a counter person.

But we get the full benefit of Mary's $12 per hour. In fact, *we can keep adding people this way until there are too many customers for one counter person to handle.* Neat, huh? Here's how it works.

$ 60	Price of 2 baskets	
- $ 20	Cost of raw materials	
- $ 16	Tom's and Mary's wages	
$ 24	**Gross margin**	
- $ 6	Counter person	
$ 18	**Tom's and Mary's contribution to the business**	

Since we already have a counter person when we hire Mary, we do not need another, so Mary's full productivity is a benefit to the company. Extend the math out for yourself, and you will see that non-core employees' productivity may often be spread out over several core employees.

Non-payroll expenses

The concept of calculating the contribution of non-payroll expenses is the same as for employees. We figure out, as best we can, how much each purchase adds to revenue. Let's start with the easiest category— Cost of Goods Sold. For baskets, this is the cost of the raw material. For now, we will assume that we do not include any payroll costs in this category. Obviously, if we do not purchase raw materials, we cannot make any baskets and our business is dead. Raw materials, then, are core expenses. We cannot do without them.

Along with core expenses are those that are not COGS but are still necessary. For example, if we sell our baskets in a store, we have to have, well, a store. That store must have certain things in it like a counter, a computer, maybe some tables and chairs and some minimum of decor. For the most part, we pay for these all at once up front. When planning for our business, we can count these as necessary.

Other expenses are necessary but ongoing. Insurance, rent, utilities, phone, and things like that fall in this category. We can't do business without them. Other expenses are completely frivolous. For example, we do not need an ivory statue in the entranceway of a basket store. As with payroll, the problem is what to do with those expenses that fall somewhere between the obviously necessary and the obviously silly.

Advertising is a good example. Could we do without advertising? Some businesses do, though it is rare. The real question is what advertising buys us in terms of increased revenue. If I run my basket business for several months with no advertising and then run an ad in the local paper and business picks up by $500 a week for a couple of weeks, I can be pretty sure that advertising is what did it. Conversely, if I run ads constantly for weeks, and then drop them for a while and business slows, I can be pretty sure it was the advertising.

Now, here's the real question. Assuming we can link our advertising expenditures to changes in revenue, was the expenditure worth it? For advertising, the calculation is easy. If the ad costs us $500 and our increased revenues amounted to $500, we broke even on that ad.

Any more revenue and we were ahead of the game. Any less and we were behind. Nothing mysterious about that, right?

Would that it were that easy to link advertising with productivity. For newspaper, radio, and TV ads, it is next to impossible to tell for sure whether they are working. We simply have no way to link them. For mailers, coupons, and other types of promotions and advertising, we at least have some way of counting how many came back in and were redeemed.

Other expenses are even harder to assess in terms of effectiveness. One of my favorite examples is cleaning. Say you hire a nightly janitorial service. Does that pay? Certainly not directly. You can't say that the $9 an hour you pay a janitor results in a certain amount of revenue. On the other hand, you can bet that if you don't hire a service and the place begins to look filthy, you will lose business.

Growth capital

When we start out on a very long car trip, we realize we cannot put enough gas in the car to get us there. No problem, because we know there are gas stations along the way. Likewise, a business can only put enough "gas in the tank" to get it to a certain point. To go farther, we have to get more gas in the form of money. This kind of money is called *growth capital*.

There are some limits to this analogy. First, while a car only uses up gasoline, a business both uses *and creates* money. Theoretically, this means a business, once launched, could sustain itself and grow without additional money from outside sources. This is more rare than one might think, though many unsuspecting people start businesses thinking they will never need to talk to another investor once they launch. To see why this is difficult to pull off, let's visit Betty the basket maker.

Betty has grown her basket-making business wisely by thinking like an entrepreneur, not a jobholder. She now has one store humming along at a good pace and realizes that she will soon reach a limit. The area she serves will not support much more business. Her presence in the market as a quality provider has discouraged competitors. They are out there, but none have been able to hurt her much. Things are looking good.

Now Betty wants to expand to another location. She has calculated the cost of opening another store and wonders how she can get the money to fund it. There are only two options. Either she uses money she has made from the first store to fund the expansion or she has to get it from somewhere else. Let's look at each scenario.

Bootstrapping

First of all, Betty analyzes what she did right in opening her first store and what she could have done better. She has developed systems that allow her to manage a single store with reasonable effort and after a couple of years, she feels she can leave the store for extended periods of time without having things fall apart. One of her employees has become the store manager, and another has been able to handle the store while the manager vacations. All in all, it looks like it is time to expand.

Betty looks at the bank account and figures that she has enough to open a new store. How does she know that? First, she tallies the amount of money that needs to be in the account of store #1. Looking at the regular ebb and flow of sales over yearlong periods of time, she calculates the lowest cash balance she can have and still fund three months of zero revenues. In other words, she has a three-month "disaster survival" fund.

Next, Betty looks back at her start-up figures for the first store. She learned, as most entrepreneurs do, that she had more expenses related to start up than she had anticipated back then. Adding them up and building in a small "fudge factor," she confirms what she suspected. She has enough cash to open another location.

What Betty has just done is called "bootstrapping." Boot strapping is simply funding a business's growth using its own earnings. It has its advantages. First, you don't have to ask anybody for money. No investors mean that you retain full control. It also means that you do not have to share your profits with others.

Before you get too excited, though, realize that bootstrapping is exceedingly hard to pull off. Most businesses require outside funding in order to grow. And even if you do manage to grow by bootstrapping, it will be difficult to achieve a rapid growth rate. Most times, count on investors.

Growing with investors

Why would anyone want to invest in your business? Choice A: they really think you are a swell person and want you to grow both financially and spiritually. Choice B: they want to make money. Hint: do not choose A.

Of course, an investor may also happen to like you and want you to grow spiritually, but he or she mostly wants to make money. Here is another fact that throws some people off. They want to make a *lot* of money. Know why? Because investing in you and me is much riskier than investing in off-the-shelf investment instruments. When entrepreneurs hear that their investors want a 40% annualized return, they often recoil in horror and refuse to even discuss terms.

Covering the reasons behind investors' desire to earn 40% on their money is beyond the scope of this book. Suffice it to say that by the time an investor has ten or so deals in his or her portfolio, five will have gone broke, three will have survived but never really taken off, and one or two will be home runs. In other words, they have to make their money off of a small percentage of their deals. If they cannot make 40% return, it is simply not worth investing.

Knowing what investors want can mean the difference between a frustrating but ultimately fruitful search for growth capital and complete failure. Knowing how to present your idea to investors so that they see what is in it for them is key.

First, remember that investors have seen it all. You and I may think our idea has never been seen, done, or even thought of. Not likely. These folks have endured years of hopeful entrepreneurs coyly giving them exclusive "insight" into the best product since ice cream. In fact, you and I will rarely come up with an idea that someone has not done before in some form. That is not a bad thing, mind you. Truly new ideas are often not good entrepreneurial bets anyway. Investors have a saying that you can always tell the pioneer—he is the one with the arrows in his back.

Second, investors are interested in your business model, not your product. You and I may be excited that we just invented the best windshield wiper blade in history, and so we want to talk and talk and talk about it. About ninety seconds in, the investor is thinking, "OK, OK. You make wiper blades. Now, how are you going to make money selling them?" Explain your product in one minute—literally. The rest of your allotted time should be spent on how you will reach customers and get them to buy your windshield wipers.

Third, resist the urge to be defensive. The investor's job is to find every possible hole in your argument. They have to. If they didn't, they would have already lost all their money on hare-brained schemes. Then where would you and I be? Know your stuff cold, respond briefly and politely to their questions, and go on to the next point. Chances are, you are going to get a lot of practice at this, because it takes *numerous* presentations to investors to find a good match.

The business plan

I laugh at academics. That is my privilege because I *am* one. Fortunately, I am not the kind who can explain how a watch works but cannot tell time. I keep at least one foot firmly planted on the ground. That philosophy has served me well over the years, but it has not always endeared me to my colleagues.

One time, I attended a conference in which two presenters gave a talk entitled, "Why business plans are completely unnecessary." I listened to their arguments, thinking this was obviously some clever title designed to promote their paper. It wasn't. They really believed that business plans were a waste of time and effort and that truly successful businesses start with no plan whatsoever. After enduring as much as I could silently, I asked them to imagine themselves as consultants rather than academics. Could they, in good conscience, advise a client to try to raise investment money without a business plan?

Their answer, as I suspected it would be, was completely lame. As they stammered and stuttered, it became clear that they had never really *asked* a real investor. They had taken some comment they had read somewhere about how many businesses "start" without a formal plan and turned it into a ridiculous overgeneralization. Can you and I take a few action steps before we write up a plan? You bet. In fact, I recommend it. Don't get caught in the "paralysis by analysis" trap. When the time comes to get serious, though, write a plan.

What should a plan contain? There is only one right answer. It should contain whatever your reader needs to decide to be a part of your success. There are a thousand books and web sites that tell you that these ten sections or those twelve topics are essential. A thousand more will tell you that it should be this many or that many pages long. Baloney. It should be whatever it needs to be to accomplish your purpose. If an investor wants notes on a napkin, do that (though I think I would be worried about doing business with that particular investor). If your investor wants a two-hundred-page spiral-bound book with color photographs and lots of charts, do that. The business plan is a tool to accomplish a specific purpose. Don't get caught up in "shoulds."

There are nonetheless a few guidelines that every plan should follow. First, make sure to write well. Take care to use proper spelling and punctuation. Format it nicely, breaking it up into readable chunks. When appropriate, use charts and graphs to bolster your argument. Make sure that you explain your business model in simple, crystal clear language. Don't leave the reader guessing what you do and how you make money doing it.

One last word on business plans. Some people regard their ideas as some big secret and the business plan as requiring White House-level security. While prudence is good, don't get carried away. First, do not put true intellectual property information in your plan. If you just discovered that baking soda mixed with another household product cures cancer, don't tell folks what that other product is. Your investors may need to know, but you don't have to tell them until well into the due diligence process.

Beyond that, most people err on the side of sharing too *little*, not too much. I have lost count of the number of people I have known over the years who had a good idea but refused to share it with anybody unless they signed a non-disclosure agreement. OK, you heard it here first. No one, repeat *no one* who can actually give you investment money will ever sign one of those. If, and this is a big "if," you get far enough along that it is absolutely necessary to share your "secret sauce," they *may* sign. Most times, it is simply not necessary to share that information at all. Your investors can usually discern whether the business model works without knowing the source code or the recipe or the place you get your fountain-of-youth water.

Now that I have convinced you not to get too worked up about non-disclosure agreements, let me suggest you temper that with some good judgment. Anything you share in a public forum becomes public in certain legal senses. Let's say I invent a gadget that both kills flies and dices tomatoes. The local paper hears about it and I explain how it works and how to make it in an interview, but do not have a patent. Jones down the road decides to manufacture and sell his version of the Amazing Flomatonator based on my idea. Can I sue Jones? Not likely, though I should consult my attorney to make sure. Once that information has been shared in a public forum, I may be out of luck. What does that have to do with my business plan? Everything. If I want to protect something I think really does have intellectual property value, I should not give it away until I have consulted an attorney who specializes in patents.

In the end, your biggest problem in growing by partnering with investors is not likely to be keeping your secret a secret. Your biggest problem will be getting enough people to read your plan. It may take dozens or even hundreds of attempts to find the right investor.

A last word on growth

Growth is good, mostly. Handle it as you would a cobra, though. Being honest with yourself about what you like to do is essential. You may start your business thinking you just want to make really great cookies and then find out that you love growing that business into a multi-million dollar enterprise. On the other hand, you may find that you just really just like to make cookies and that the extra income you get is enough for your purposes. Remember, you can't achieve someone else's goal—it has to be yours and yours only.

If you do decide to grow in a big way, allow for mistakes. Each stage of growth requires a new set of rules and a new way of thinking. The trip is exciting but more than a little scary. In the end, you will probably be glad you chose to grow prudently instead of building a house of cards.

9 Maximizing the Value of Your Business

"Price is what you pay.
Value is what you get."
—*Warren Buffett*

 I once had lunch with an entrepreneur who was getting ready to expand his operation by purchasing a local business. His business was making awnings for mobile homes and trailers. As we conversed over a cup of coffee at the local diner, he described his ambivalent feelings toward the purchase. On the one hand, he was excited about growing. On the other, he was saddened by the situation of the seller.

The seller, a likable sort, was very proud of the business he had built. Thirty years before, he had decided to go out on his own. To his credit, the business had survived these many years. He had counted on the business to fund his retirement. Now, nearing seventy, he was ready to reap the rewards of his labor.

Puzzled at this point about why he was saddened, I asked the entrepreneur to explain.

"Frank (the seller) thinks he has something of value. In reality, he is selling a job. How much would you pay for a job?"

Still confused, I asked Jim (the buyer) what he meant.

"Frank has worked sixty hours a week for thirty years. He *is* his business. When Frank goes home at night, his business goes with him. Sure, he's had some employees over the years, but the lion's share of work has been done by Frank and Frank alone. Because he has been able to pay his personal bills all these years, he thinks he has a solid business. And in a sense, he does. Or at least he does as long as he is there working. The problem is that his business is a value to no one but him. It is no more than a job.

"I want the business because he has a building, some inventory, and a few tools that would be useful to me. When we first talked about this transaction, I added up the value of his inventory and tools and made an offer. Frank was stunned. 'What about goodwill?' he asked. 'This business has existed for thirty years, good times and bad.' I showed him the numbers he had given me for the last three years of business. Then I explained that while the business had indeed paid his bills, it had done little else. I might pick up a few customers, and I factored that into my offer, but it was nothing like what Frank expected. In the end, he realized that I was right. No one would pay him what he expected because the cash flow generated by the business would not support it."

Jim knew what Frank had only just learned. Burn this into your memory. *A business is only worth what it can generate in positive cash flow.* When Jim ran the numbers, he realized that he would have to replace Frank. Once Frank's salary was being paid to someone else, there was nothing left for the business itself. Jim would have a location and a few tangible assets, but it was up to him to build a revenue stream that would make the business truly valuable.

How many people out there are in the same situation? I shudder to think. Many, if not most, small business owners have succeeded in creating a job for themselves. The problem with a job is that when you quit, you stop getting paid. Not knowing the difference between building a business and creating a job for yourself is deadly.

What makes a business valuable?

One more time: *a business is only worth what it can generate in positive cash flow.* How does this affect your retirement plans? First, it means that if having a secure and steady income in your retirement years is a goal, you will not get there by creating a job for yourself. Like any other job, the income stops when you stop showing up for work. A business is not the same thing as a job, though few people really understand this.

Let's break this down by visiting another basket maker—Jane. First, imagine Jane has created a business that has a steady positive cash flow. Imagine further that she pays herself from the business's income. For the sake of simplicity, let's say this is her full-time occupation—she holds no other job. A typical month's cash flow might look like this:

$	10,000	Revenue
- $	3,000	COGS
- $	6,000	Administrative costs
$	1,000	**Positive cash flow**

That means $1,000 a month is added to the business's checking account. If this happens every month, Jane's cash grows by $12,000 a year, not including what she takes home in salary. If she is smart, she will treat that $12,000 as the *business's* money—not hers. This sounds like a triviality, but treating your business as a separate entity helps instill fiscal discipline.

Further, lets assume Jane is paying herself about what she would have to pay someone else to do what she does. In other words, her salary is at market. Nearing the age she wants to retire, Jane starts figuring out how to sell the basket business and live off the proceeds.

There are two kinds of proceeds from the sale. First, she will take all the cash she has accumulated. If she has worked the business for five years, that amounts to $60,000—a nice sum, but certainly not enough to retire on.

Second, she will get paid by someone for the business itself. The business has a few tangible assets—things you can put your hands on, like some counters and workbenches. These do not add up to much, though, and are not a big consideration in someone's purchasing the business. The most liquid asset, the cash in the checking account, is going with Jane. So why would anyone want the business at all?

Martha comes along and is in a similar situation to Jane's a few years ago. She wants her own business and recognizes that it is a heck of a lot easier to buy an ongoing concern than it is to start from scratch. If she plans to work in the business and take a salary like Jane did, the "value" of the business itself to her is the "extra" cash flow—the part we described above as belonging to the business. That amounts to $1000 a month. If all she got in the deal were a job, she could get one in another basket shop and avoid all the hassles of running a business.

So how could Martha be justified in paying to get that $1,000 a month ($12,000 a year)? Think of it as you would any other investment. It is an income stream generated by a certain amount of money parked somewhere. A savings account does the same thing. If I put $10,000 in such an account, and the rate is 2%, I earn $200 a year (forget compounding for now). If Martha pays $600,000 for Jane's business, she earns the same as she would in a saving account.

$$\frac{\$12,000 \text{ a year cash flow}}{\$600,000 \text{ investment}} = 2\%$$

This figure is called *cash-on-cash return,* and it is absolutely critical to understand. In this scenario, Martha would be crazy to purchase. She can put her money in a savings account, which is safe, and earn as much money as she would in this business, which is risky. Clearly, $600,000 is too much to pay. $300,000, is too—4% return can be earned elsewhere more safely. So Martha has to lower her offer to the point where it earns her the return she feels is justified for the risk. Let's say she settles on 10% return.

An offer of $120,000 would result in a cash-on-cash return of 10% for Martha as long as the business continues to perform as it has.

$$\frac{\$12,000 \text{ a year cash flow}}{\$120,000 \text{ investment}} = 10\%$$

But what about Jane? The truth is, $180,000 (the $60,000 cash she has accumulated plus the $120,000 purchase price of the business) will last as long as a June frost. Even if she could invest it somewhere at 4% interest, she would only make about $9,000 a year.

Ouch.

How did Jane get fooled? She worked hard for five years and made a good living. Now she faces the grim prospect of having little or no retirement income. In order to understand how she got into this predicament, we need to look at some choices she made when she was building the business.

Employee or entrepreneur?

When Jane first started her business, she wisely watched every penny. Figuring that employees were expensive, she kept payroll to a minimum and did most things herself. This saved her quite a bit of money, she thought. Since she paid herself a salary, she did not need to draw any more from the business's account for her personal use. She thought she was saving $1,000 a month as well, which she was. Kind of.

The business grew and gained a solid reputation for great quality and customer service. In every respect, Jane thought she had built a valuable business. And, looking from the outside, she had. Without realizing it, though, Jane had limited the business's growth by being an employee more than an entrepreneur.

As the number of customers grew, Jane became more involved in servicing them than in getting more. She did not consciously choose to avoid growing—it just happened. Scurrying around making sure things went well and still making lots of baskets herself, she barely had time to breathe, much less think about how to grow the business. She did not notice that she had reached an invisible ceiling. Jane was no longer an entrepreneur. She was an employee of the business she created. What could she have done to prevent this? Let's go back to our original basket maker, Betty.

Betty started out much the same as Jane. She too was consumed at first with the day-to-day activities of running her business. As each day saw more and more customers, she dove in to do all the things that needed to get done herself. One day, she sat down over a cup of coffee and went over her sales figures. She realized that though she had worked hard for several months, the number of customers had not grown. Unlike Jane, Betty realized she had hit a limit.

"This can't be right," she thought. "If anything, I have put in more hours and worked more efficiently. I sure *feel* busier."

Then Betty remembered why she started this business in the first place. She hated having a job. Though she always enjoyed working, she despised answering to a boss and having her life blocked out by the dictates of a time clock. Suddenly, she laughed out loud. She had managed to create for herself the very thing she hated. At that moment, Betty became an entrepreneur.

The first thing she did was look at her numbers. Cash flow was good. Month after month, she put back $1,000. She also paid herself a reasonable amount for a salary. The $1,000 was not enough to hire a full-time person, but she was close to having enough for a part-timer. She decided to reduce her own salary by $200 a month, combine it with the $1,000, and use the total of $1,200 a month to hire someone.

Betty then resolved to stop making baskets herself. The baskets she had been making could be done by the new hire and she could spend that time doing something else. But what? Well, she did have some designs in mind that she had not had time to get down on paper. She had also read in a trade magazine about Web 2.0. Though she did not understand it completely, she knew it supported social networking that allowed small businesses like hers to advertise in a cost-effective way. Having some extra time would allow her to take a course offered at the local community college and to explore other ways of promoting her business.

At first, things were tough. The new person needed some coaching, and she did not really like having to watch her personal budget so closely. Sometimes she wished for that $200 back, but she held onto the thought that this was best in the long run. It was. Within six months, her sales revenues were showing steady growth. The new hire was working out well and would soon be moved to full-time. Her cash flow had improved, and she had enough money to raise her own salary again. After some thought, she decided to only increase it by $100.

Betty stayed busy, but not frantic. She designed more baskets, which were proving to have wide appeal to her customers. She had established an Internet social network that included customers from all over the world, mostly referred by existing customers. Things were looking good.

This tale of Two basket makers is even more instructive when retirement time rolls around. Betty will continue to build a business that creates an ever-increasing positive cash flow. She may even open other locations using the same business model. When she decides to sell the business, it will be many times more valuable than the one built by Jane.

Valuation

Above, I said that a business is worth what it generates in positive cash flow. But cash flow has two components if we look at it over a period of time. First, there is the steady cash flow we saw in Jane's business. Since she has hit a ceiling, any purchaser of the business will figure his or her cash flow will remain the same over the next few years. Her *growth rate* is zero. In other words, the purchaser is buying an asset with a fixed return, like a savings account. Betty has an extra advantage. Since her business is growing, the buyer can factor in a higher cash flow in the coming years. The promise of growth itself is valuable.

Let's be cautious here. The final word on any business purchase is the market. No matter how clever this method seems to you and me, it is the buyer who ultimately sets the price. However, there are good reasons for the buyer to use this or some similar method. If he or she expects to gain from the purchase, more money has to come back than went in. If the offer is too high, the buyer will not get an adequate return on the investment. If the offer is too low, the seller won't take it.

Finding buyers

Selling a business is quite a bit different from selling a decorative basket. First, not as many people want a business. Second, it costs more money. Third, people buy baskets to enjoy, but they buy businesses to make money. At one time, the brass ring was the Initial Public Offering (IPO) where a company sold stock to the public. This type of "sale" is exceedingly difficult these days, as the rules governing IPOs have become almost impossible to satisfy. Further, it takes many, many years to build a business big enough to take public.

Another option is finding a private individual or group of individuals who wish to own this particular type of business. This type of sale may include seller financing, whereby the seller takes monthly payments over a period of time. The seller gets an income without having to work anymore.

Selling to employees is similar to selling to private individuals. The buyer may be a single employee or the employees as a whole that combine to form a buying entity.

All of the above are viable options, but perhaps the most straightforward type of sale is to a larger company. Betty could be approached by, or generate the interest of, a large novelty items firm or some other business that wanted to expand its product line or eliminate her as competition.

No system, no sale

While the cash flow of a business is the primary driver of its value, that concept requires clarification. It is the *future* cash flow that really matters. What happened in the past only gives the buyer something to estimate future earnings by. Absent some confidence that those earnings will continue, there is no reason to buy an existing business. What gives a buyer the confidence that he or she is buying a business that will continue churning out cash? First, let's examine what will *not* work.

Any business in which the owner is also the primary employee is not a good candidate for sale. Jane is up to her eyeballs in work but has built no lasting value. Day to day, it is Jane that makes the place go. Without her, the basket business grinds to a halt. She tried taking a vacation once, but when she returned two weeks later, she found a disaster waiting. Raw materials had not been ordered, customers were fuming over late orders, and one key employee had quit. She vowed never again to go away for more than a day.

Even if Jane had built the business up to a healthy cash flow, she could have the same problem if she *as a person* is the core of operations.

Buyers want a business that cranks out cash irrespective of the particular people in charge. If a rogue asteroid hits Jane, their investment is kaput.

Betty on the other hand thinks like an entrepreneur. An entrepreneur builds businesses of lasting value by creating business *systems.* A system allows things to happen predictably without a particular person having to do them.

The simplest example of a business system is a to-do list. Imagine that Betty has created a to-do list for each day of the month. Certain things need to be done on a monthly, weekly, or daily basis. If Betty were incapacitated, you or I could take that list and do a passable job of running her business. We may make a few mistakes, and there may be some things on the list for which we do not have the requisite skills, but all in all, the business could run.

Contrast this to a business that is all in Jane's head. You or I walk in to run the business even for a day and there is nothing to go on. Papers are strewn about, people are asking for things that cannot be located, and employees seem to be lost. It would take us weeks or even months to learn how to make things hum again.

Many people resist this kind of methodical approach to business, preferring to run things "by the seat of the pants." The problem is that your seat is in close proximity to your brain when you do things that way. It makes us feel good to think that we are indispensable. Watch people who run businesses sometime. Many are taking calls constantly, solving every little problem that crops up. They complain about being harried, but you can tell that down deep, they love being needed. Being needed in that way, though, is shallow and counterproductive.

My advice to such folks is to trade the temporary satisfaction of being indispensable for the long-lasting satisfaction of having a solid business that can be sold. At some point, being needed like that gets old. Farther on in life, you may want to enjoy the income without the work. And if you don't think you will, ask someone in his or her eighties.

Beyond the to-do list

Running a business by systems does not mean blindly following a set of prescriptions. Things change, and a business must change in response to or in anticipation of events that affect it. Your role as an entrepreneur rather than an employee is to manage those systems wisely. If you are constantly solving "right now" type problems, you simply have no time or energy to improve upon your business model.

The general rule for system building is simple. Anything you have to do twice needs a system. For example, Betty realized that if she were to follow a standard routine for every recurring task, she would not need to rethink it every time. It is said that Einstein had five sets of clothes, all the same. When asked why, he replied, "Not having to decide saves me thirty seconds a day." For Einstein, that meant thirty more seconds to think about relativity. I don't recommend Einstein's fashion strategy, but you get the point.

The easiest candidates for systematization in your business are what I call "toothbrushing" jobs. We may occasionally skip shaving or some other daily-care routine, but most of us brush those teeth religiously. If we don't, our conversation partners may wonder why. Not to mention that icky, grimy feeling we all have first thing in the morning. Bleccchhh...

Betty started by finding toothbrushing tasks, things like unlocking the door at 9:00am, turning the closed/open sign around, setting up the register, and so forth. She created a list that not only made sense to her, but to her employees. In fact, just to be safe, she wrote the items so that her grandmother could understand them.

Next, Betty found those tasks that were not quite so routine, but nonetheless occurred regularly. Ordering raw materials and checking on office supplies came to mind first, followed by things like rearranging the sales floor and updating the web site.

Everything so far was part of regular operations—those things that would disrupt business if left undone. Now Betty paused to think of things that added to the business—things that could be overlooked without immediately being noticed. For example, she knew that a little over half her new business came from referrals. She designed a card that the counter person could give to every customer that made it easy to refer friends. She also created a clever way to get customers to visit the social networking site she had created by giving away a basket in a drawing.

In the end, Betty had systems for every major activity in the store. Now let's see how that helped her get an investor.

What investors really want

A few years ago, there was a movie entitled, "What Women Want." A chauvinistic executive is suddenly able to hear the thoughts of nearby females. His ability to see into the minds of the opposite sex causes him to realize how limited his perspective has been.

Betty underwent a similar transformation by attending investor meetings. She found a local group of investors who met periodically to hear entrepreneurs present business ideas for investment. By listening closely to the questions they asked and noting the things to which they responded positively, she was able to come up with several new insights.

First, she noticed that many investors grew impatient when the entrepreneur spent a long time talking about the product. Most seemed anxious to move on to the financial projections. During one meeting, she overheard an investor whispering to a friend, "OK, OK, he makes widgets. How is he going to make money?"

Second, she began to see that investors were skeptical of "percent of market" arguments. Many entrepreneurs told stories of how all they had to do was get "1%" of the total market. Investors *skewered* these presenters. They wanted to know how the business planned to get real, live, breathing customers, not how MBAs calculate market share.

Third, Betty began to see why investors wanted such a large return. Many of the business ideas she saw presented were far from sure bets. She could see a huge upside potential for some of them, but only if certain things happened. Betty began to appreciate how hard it was to pick the winners.

Retiring with peace of mind

Betty began to lay plans for her retirement. She knew in a few years she would not want to spend all her time running her business. She also knew she wanted to really *enjoy* retirement, not worry constantly about cutting corners to pay the bills. After learning about what investors wanted from a business, she set out to grow in earnest.

The first three or four locations were hard. Betty had to refine her systems and account for some differences in location that she had not anticipated. By the fifth, she was getting into a rhythm. Her investors were happy, and she was ready to go for another round of financing. This round would get her to twenty stores. She had already been approached by a larger chain but felt in no hurry to sell. Betty felt confident that she could wait for the right offer. She knew what amount of money per month she wanted to make after retiring and the amount she needed to make in a sale to have that happen.

Before you get overwhelmed, let's stop. Betty's story is one out of thousands of possibilities. Many people simply supplement their income with a part-time business and put the money into other investments. Some build family businesses for security in the future. Others build an income stream from intellectual property such as books, videos, or patents.

No matter what your choice, I want you to understand one thing. *It is possible to build a prosperous and secure future by learning to build a business.* No one plan fits everyone, but there is one plan that is sure to fail: doing nothing. I believe that counting solely on traditional retirement plans is highly risky. Supplementing or even replacing your income with a solid, well-built business can mean the difference between poverty and prosperity.

The problem is not just one of making *more* money. The issue is what kind of asset provides the income you want and need in the future. Paper retirements such as stocks, bonds, and mutual funds are fine, as far as they go. But what if rampant inflation kicks in? Will they keep pace? What if fund managers get taken by another huge Ponzi scheme? What then?

Knowing how to build a business gives you the wherewithal to weather the storm while others have only one solution—find a job, hope you don't lose it, and put some money away. I sincerely hope the people who do only that fare well in the coming years. Frankly, I have my doubts. As for you and me, we will have something that gives us strength through all the inevitable challenges the future may hold—knowledge. To put a new spin on an old phrase, don't give me a fish; teach me *how* to fish.

10 The Learning Never Stops

"Learning is a treasure that will follow its owner everywhere."

—*Chinese Proverb*

Hopefully, you now have an appreciation of what it takes to start a new business. Let's return to the question of why. I began this book with the admonition that we are facing tough times ahead. Our leaders have squandered our wealth, lied about the state of the economy, and used every excuse in the book to enrich themselves at our expense. Don't expect that to change. Until the majority of Americans understand what has been done to them and refuse to take any more, we have to deal with the situation as it is, like it or not.

What does that mean? It means arming ourselves with knowledge. For all the doom and gloom I may seem to dwell on, I remain optimistic. I want you to be an optimist as well, but a reality-based optimist. Those of us who devote ourselves to learning to create our own wealth, open ourselves to the new opportunities this crisis presents, and work to build the kind of character that wealth-building requires will come out of all of this smelling like a rose. Those who do not will smell like, well, not a rose. Here is my view of the realities of the next decade and beyond.

Who will prosper and who will suffer

No one can predict the future with certainty, but we all can predict the future within certain bounds. If we could not, we would not survive a sunny afternoon. We know that if we plant a seed and water the young plant that springs forth, we will have food to eat later. We know that if we exercise today, we will feel better tomorrow. We know that if we spend our paychecks on beer and cigarettes or gamble our savings away in a casino, we will wind up broke or worse.

It is harder to predict the future when it comes to the economy in general, because it is much more complicated. Complicated, but not a complete mystery. We know that certain policies lead to disaster. Central economic planning, for example, has never worked and never will. Not only has history provided us numerous examples of the folly of pure socialism, we know *why* it does not work. No single person or set of persons can possibly allocate resources effectively. The billions upon billions of decisions that make up an economy work to increase wealth for all when people are left to decide—on their own—what is best for them and theirs. When someone tries to convince you the market is not "fair," grab your wallet. What they mean is that they want to impose on you their idea of fair. In the end, that always means taking your money and giving it to someone else.

Ours is not a pure centrally planned economy—yet. I hope beyond hope that it does not become one. If it does, we will have squandered the precious gift of freedom our Founders gave us. And if we do allow that to happen, we deserve it. As long as we have the right to speak our minds and vote our conscience without fear of reprisal, there remains the hope of stopping our precipitous slide toward tyranny.

In the meantime, we have to deal with the realities of an economy that is neither pure socialism nor pure capitalism. Those who learn how the rules are changing and how to build wealth in spite of the government and all the huge companies that are in bed with the government will, with patience and perseverance, probably come out all right. The rest, I fear, will get clobbered, never understanding why.

Let me reiterate something I said at the beginning of our journey together. I am not a fan of *any* major political party. My views of limited government would be described by most as libertarian, though I do not identify with the Libertarian Party. I love freedom, and I love humanity. In my view, when people are left to their own devices with minimal interference, they may make mistakes, but on the whole they will prosper. Here are some things that I think are going to louse that freedom up over the next few years.

Fiat money

The dollar is only worth the faith that people have in our government's ability to pay its debts. Politicians have essentially made us a nation of debtors. The social programs and wars that seem so compelling at the time we start them become a millstone around our collective necks as the bill comes due. So far, this teetering house of cards has not fallen completely. The year 2008 was a wake-up call as our banking system came within hours of freezing up completely.

What has government's response been? To do more, a *lot* more, of what got us into trouble in the first place. At the time I wrote the first edition, we were about to inject $7-8 *trillion* dollars into our economy. (If you want to have some fun, figure out how many Corvettes that is.) Lord only knows how much more has been pumped in both on and off the government's books.

What is the justification for this? Politicians think the problem is that people are not spending enough money. Resurrecting Keynes, they believe that by giving people money to spend, everything will be all right. Let's keep in mind that this "money" is created out of thin air. It is not backed by gold or silver and has no intrinsic value whatsoever.

Only a few things can happen with that much fake money floating around. The first and least likely scenario is that the government will wake up, realize it is incompetent to manage the economy and remove itself from the economic system altogether. Don't hold your breath.

Another hopeful but unlikely scenario is that government will pull back spending at just the right rate to ease inflation, the inevitable result of its current policies. The current administration has reformed (essentially taken over) health care, regulated (nationalized) our financial institutions, and wants to tax (punish) all those terrible people who make too much money. Don't look for either party to pull back on spending in any significant way.

In my view, we face one of two broad scenarios. The first is a complete disaster. Our government continues to pile debt on debt and print money until people one day stop believing that those green pieces of paper we carry have any value. History shows that when people lose faith in fiat currency, which always happens eventually, the effects are quick and brutal. People who hold their wealth in the form of paper money are wiped out instantly through hyperinflation as the government frantically prints more money in the vain hope that lack of spending is the problem. Those who hold gold and silver or other tangible assets like real estate and solid businesses are able to survive and sometimes even prosper as the price of those holdings skyrockets.

The second scenario is not any prettier, but also not quite so quick. Inflation kicks in and the wealth we *think* we hold is eaten away. So we have a lot of money in numeric terms, but steadily lose buying power.

In some ways this scenario is more sinister than the first because if we look only at the *numbers*, we think we are getting richer. We get annual raises, our stocks go up in value (as measured in paper dollars), and we barely notice the steady decline in our buying power. Our government *hopes* this one prevails. It allows them to continue to spend, spend, spend without having anyone notice that they are just postponing the inevitable collapse of our fiat money.

Government "regulation"

Not once, with the possible exception of Congressman Ron Paul, have I ever heard a politician tell us the truth about what is happening. Instead, you and I have witnessed the most revolting display of finger-pointing in history. The vast majority of businesspeople are honest and hard-working. A tiny fraction of them, the Enrons of this world, engage in the kind of shenanigans that gets so much attention in the press. When things go wrong, politicians invariably respond with a call for more "regulation."

The problem with regulation is that it sounds good. People do bad things, and they should be punished, or so goes the argument. Who could disagree with that? Certainly not me, at least when the proposition is stated that way. But we all know that this is not the way regulation works. Regulation serves to give politicians the power to affect the income of businesspeople. Rather than customers deciding who prospers and who doesn't based on buying decisions, elected officials make it harder for opponents and easier for supporters to win in the marketplace. It is a racket, and should be recognized for what it is.

Even if one agrees in principle that certain things should be regulated, like say the amount of lead in toys, politicians inevitably gravitate toward solutions that sound fierce and fair but which have unintended consequences, most of them bad. Every regulation has a cost of compliance, which is obvious. Those affected have to fill out paperwork, get things approved, and hire people who do nothing buy satisfy reams of regulation.

Other distortions in the market are less obvious, but just as destructive. In some cases, small businesses are crushed, as was the case in the "lead-in-toys" scare recently. In others, innovation is squelched as the government requires layer after layer of testing and approval. In some cases, some good has been done, but the overall effect is the empowerment of government bureaucrats at the expense of honest people trying to improve their lot in life by creating value for others.

And finally, us

Yes, friends, I pledged that I would tell you the truth as best I could. And the bitter truth is that we as a people have lost our way. We sue each other over every perceived injustice no matter how trivial. We depend on our government to fix things we should be fixing ourselves. We want everybody to have a house, live comfortably in retirement, and get taken care of when sick *no matter what decisions they make that contribute to their misery.*

The bill has come due, and we no longer have the option of putting off paying. Like me, you may be fond of bashing politicians. Fine. Have fun. But in the end, the question is not what *they* are going to do. The question is what *you* are going to do.

Why starting your own business is the answer

No matter how bad things get, we human beings need each other. By making yourself valuable to other people, you participate in the one activity that makes us what we are as human beings. No other animal has even close to our capacity to think, cooperate, and prosper the way we do.

If things get bad, knowing how to build a business may save your neck. If things *don't* go bad, you will *still* have developed the capacity to increase your financial well-being. In the process, you will probably come closer to doing what you really want to do as well.

Why am I so confident that entrepreneurship is the answer? Simple. Knowing how to create value and exchange it with others is the basis of *all* business. Those who know only how to hold a job may be bright and industrious, but without the entrepreneur who builds the business they work in, they are lost. You can choose to remain someone who relies on others for a living or learn to rely on yourself. That does not necessarily mean quitting your job, but it sure as heck means knowing what to do if your job quits you.

If the stock market crashes completely, jobholders may have no place to turn. You will. If that piece of paper in your wallet becomes worthless, people who provide things of value to others will get paid in some other form. Jobholders may not. While others are scampering about wondering what to do, you will be looking for ways to capitalize on the mountain of opportunities that always accompany an upheaval. If former jobholders are lucky, you may hire them to help you build your business. When the flood comes, you will have spent your time building a boat. They will be hiding under a banana leaf.

An invitation

You have within you the capacity to see the truth. We all do. If you want to survive and prosper in the coming years, lift the veil and see the world for what it is—a wonderful but extremely unforgiving place. Develop your capacity to cut through the nonsense you read in the paper and see on the "shouting heads" shows. Find that part of you that is strong, confident, willing to learn, and courageous.

This book is meant to get you started in the right direction. I hope it has. But if you are really serious about giving you and your loved ones a real nest egg to replace the one that just got broken, learn everything you can about money and business. As noted in the Foreword, I provide online courses and will be writing more books, but I am not the only voice out there urging people to wake up. Read differing points of view and sort through them using your own intelligence and judgment. Make mistakes, grand mistakes that allow you to learn and grow. Get off the bench and into the game. Even if I never meet you, we will live together in spirit because we answered "yes" to the question life asks us, "Are you *really* ready to live?"

References

Adler, Mortimer J. (1978). *Aristotle For Everybody*. New York, NY: Touchstone.

Allen, David (2004). *Getting Things Done: The Art of Stress-Free Productivity*. New York, NY: Penguin Books.

Baddeley, Alan (2004). *Your Memory: A User's Guide*. Buffalo, NY: Firefly Books.

Bhide, Amar V. (2000). *The Origin and Evolution of New Businesses*. New York, NY: Oxford University Press.

Branden, Nathaniel (1997). *The Art of Living Consciously*. New York, NY: Fireside.

Bureau of Labor Statistics, http://www.bls.gov/opub/mlr/2004/07/art2full.pdf.

Colvin, Geoff (2008). *Talent Is Overrated*. New York, NY: Penguin Press.

Csikszenthmihalyi, Mihaly (1990). *Flow: The Psychology of Optimal Experience*. New York, NY: Harper & Row Publishers, Inc.

Frankl, Viktor E. (1988). *The Will To Meaning*. New York, NY: Penguin Group.

Gold Silver News. goldsilver.com.

Jackson, Susan A., and Csikszentmihalyi, Mihaly. (1999). *Flow In Sports: The Keys to Optimal Experiences and Performances*. Champaign, IL: Human Kinetics.

Jeffers, Susan, Ph.D. (1987). *Feel the Fear and Do It Anyway*. New York, NY: Random House Publishing Group.

Kiyosaki, Robert T. with Lechter, Sharon L. (1998). *Rich Dad, Poor Dad*. New York, NY: Warner Books, Inc.

Maloney, Michael (2008). *Guide to Investing in Gold and Silver.* New York, NY: Hachette Book Group USA.

Reynolds, Paul D., Hay, Michael, and Camp, S. Michael (1999). *Global Entrepreneurship Monitor.* Kansas City: Kauffman Center for Entrepreneurial Leadership.

Shakespeare, William (2003). *Hamlet.* New Haven: Yale University Press.

Social Security Administration, http://www.ssa.gov/history/ratios.html.

About the Author

Terry W. Noel is an Associate Professor of Management and Quantitative Methods at Illinois State University where he teaches classes in both Entrepreneurship and Management.

Dr. Noel's business background includes farming, business ownership, sales management, and consulting. He earned his doctorate from the University of Colorado at Boulder in 1997.

Dr. Noel's experience includes managing the deal flow for a $1 million student venture fund and serving as a "Hot Seat Coach" for entrepreneurs seeking funding from a consortium of angel investors and venture capitalists. He often speaks to groups on the topics of motivation and goal setting.

Dr. Noel's work has been published in such places as *The Academy of Management Journal*, the *Journal of Management Education*, and the *Journal of Entrepreneurship Education*. His research focuses on the process of entrepreneurial learning and how entrepreneurial thinking can benefit both start-ups and established organizations.

www.ingramcontent.com/pod-product-compliance
Lightning Source LLC
Chambersburg PA
CBHW051520170526
45165CB00002B/542